May each page of this coloring book be a gateway to a world of dreams and creativity. Have fun coloring and let your imagination soar high!

Ana Souza 2024

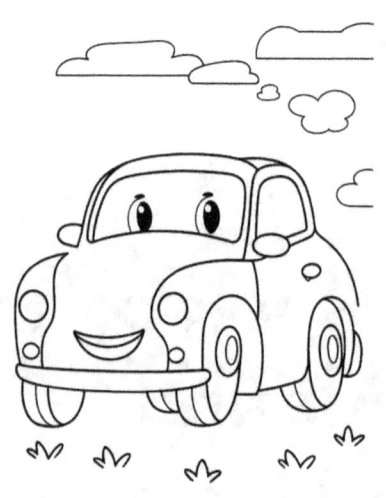
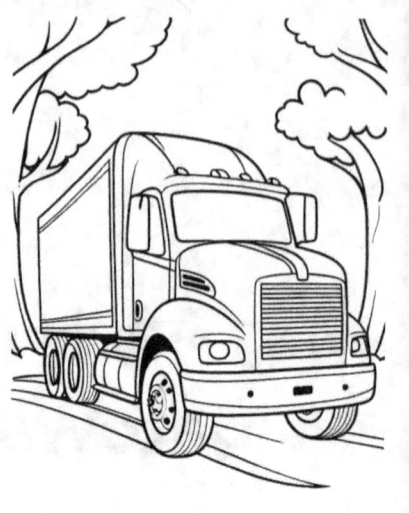

This Book Belongs To:

_____

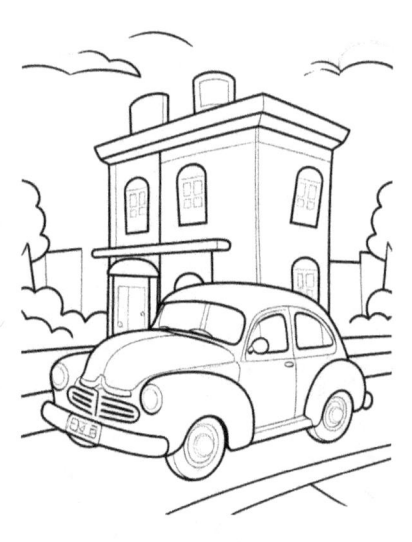

Ana Souza A .S. P.

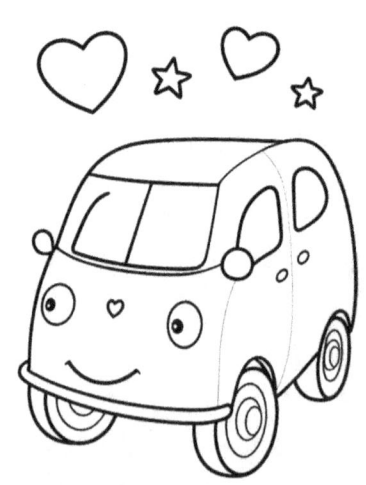

ALL RIGHTS RESERVED ©

No part of this publication may be reproduced, distributed, or transmitted in any form or by any means, including photocopyng recording or other electronic or mechanical methods, without the prior written permission of the publisher, except for brief quotations incorporated in critical reviews and other spedific noncommercial uses. Any unauthorized replica of this work is prohibited.

A.S.P.©
ANA SOUZA PUBLICATIONS

Test Color Page

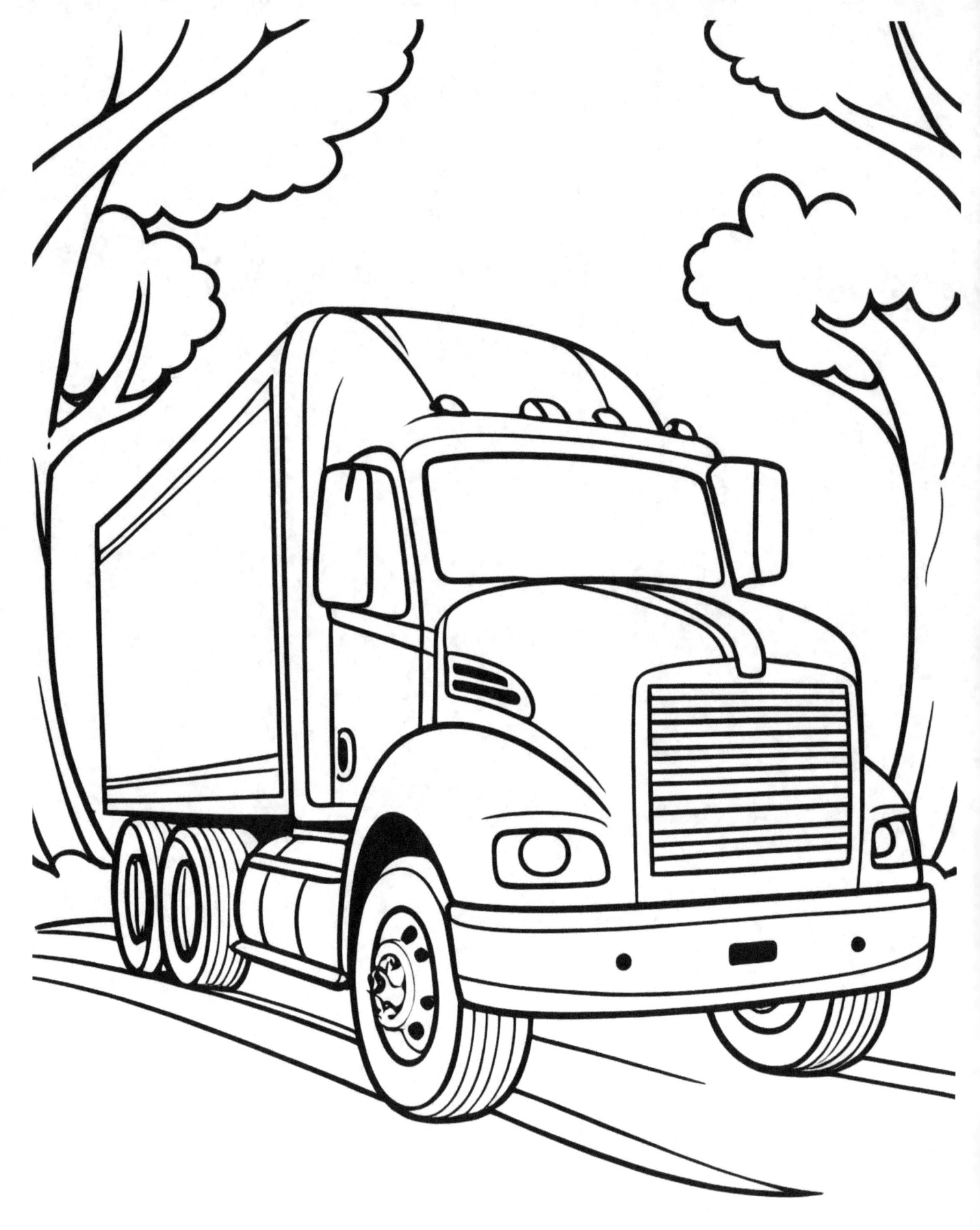

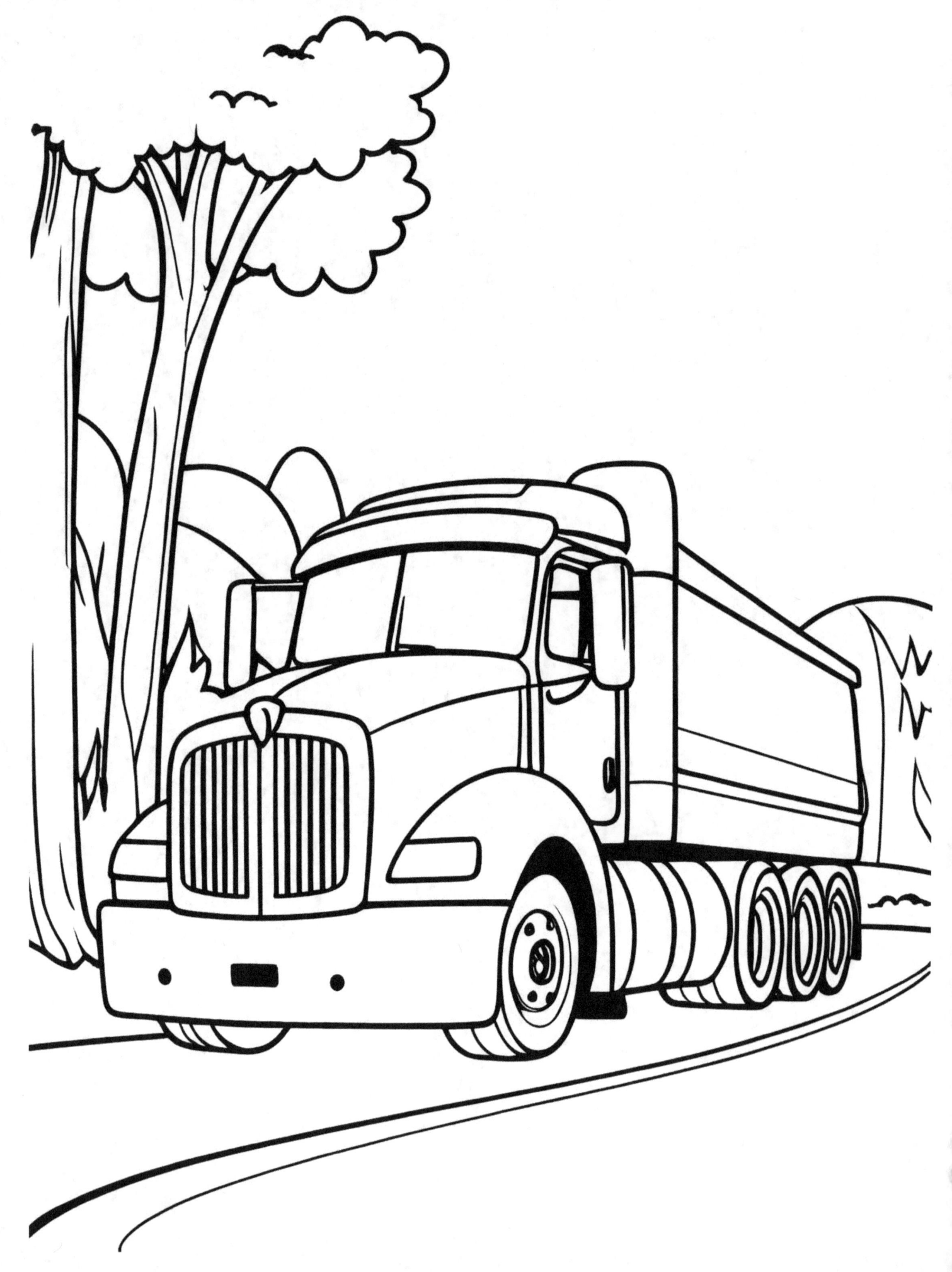

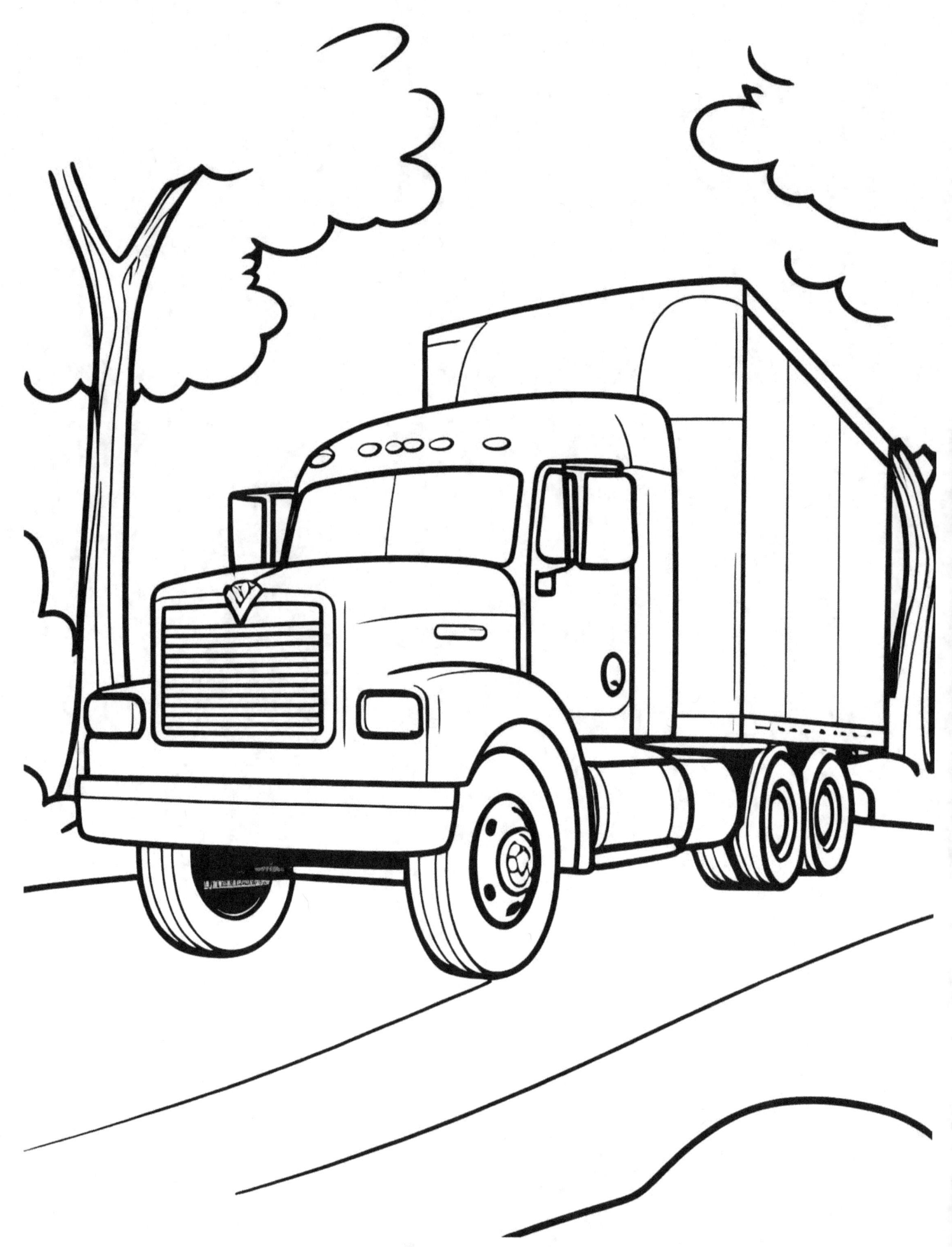

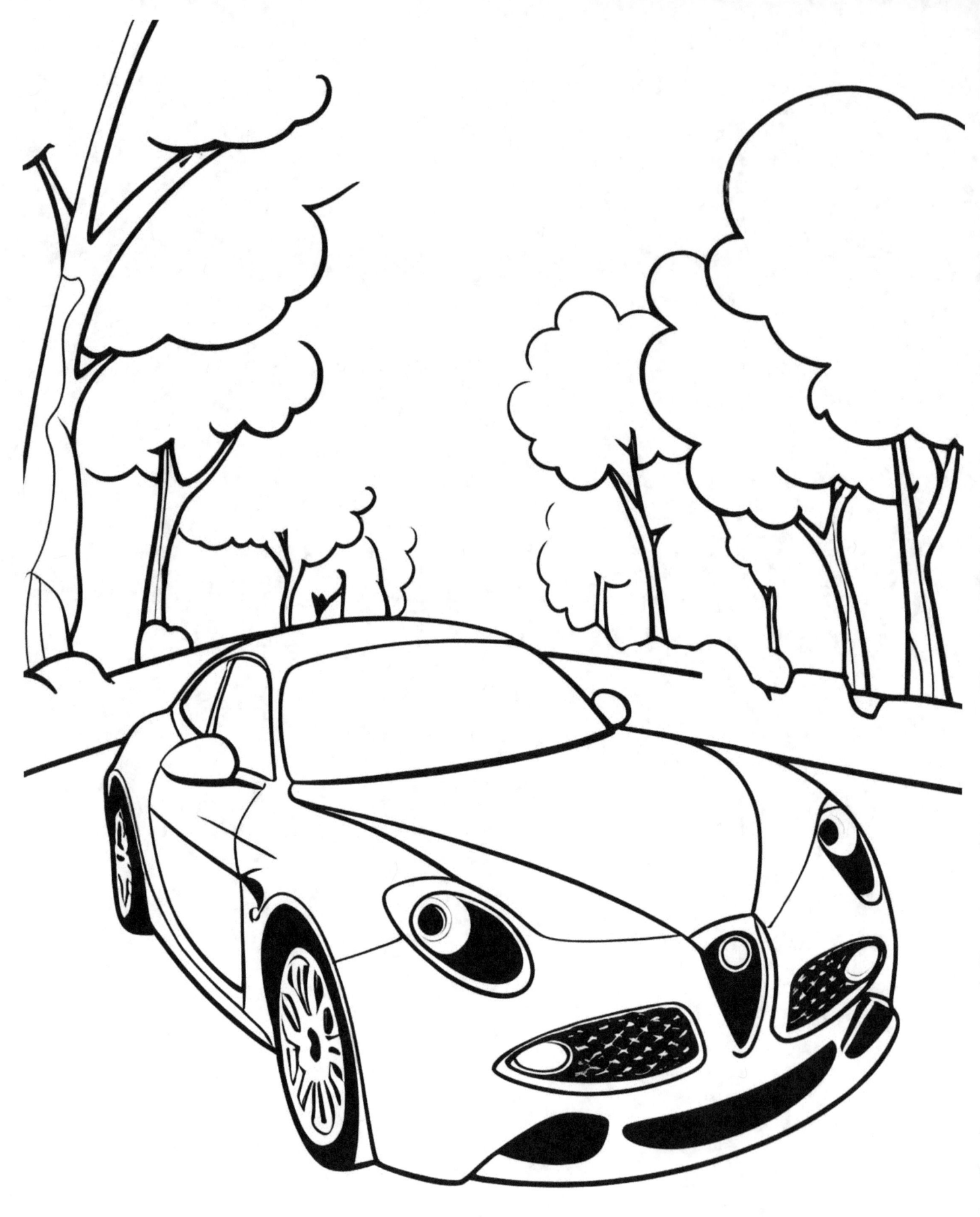

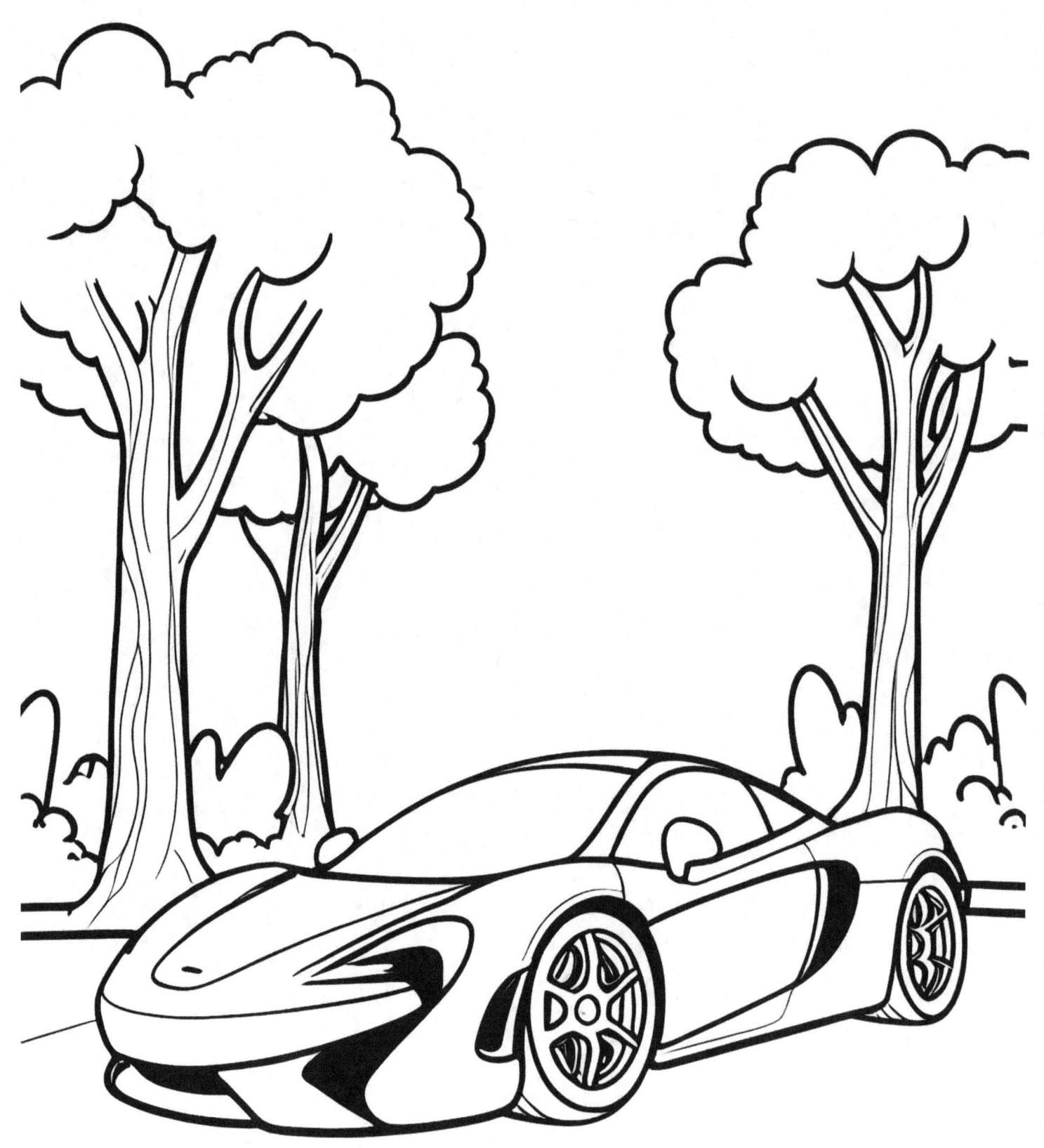

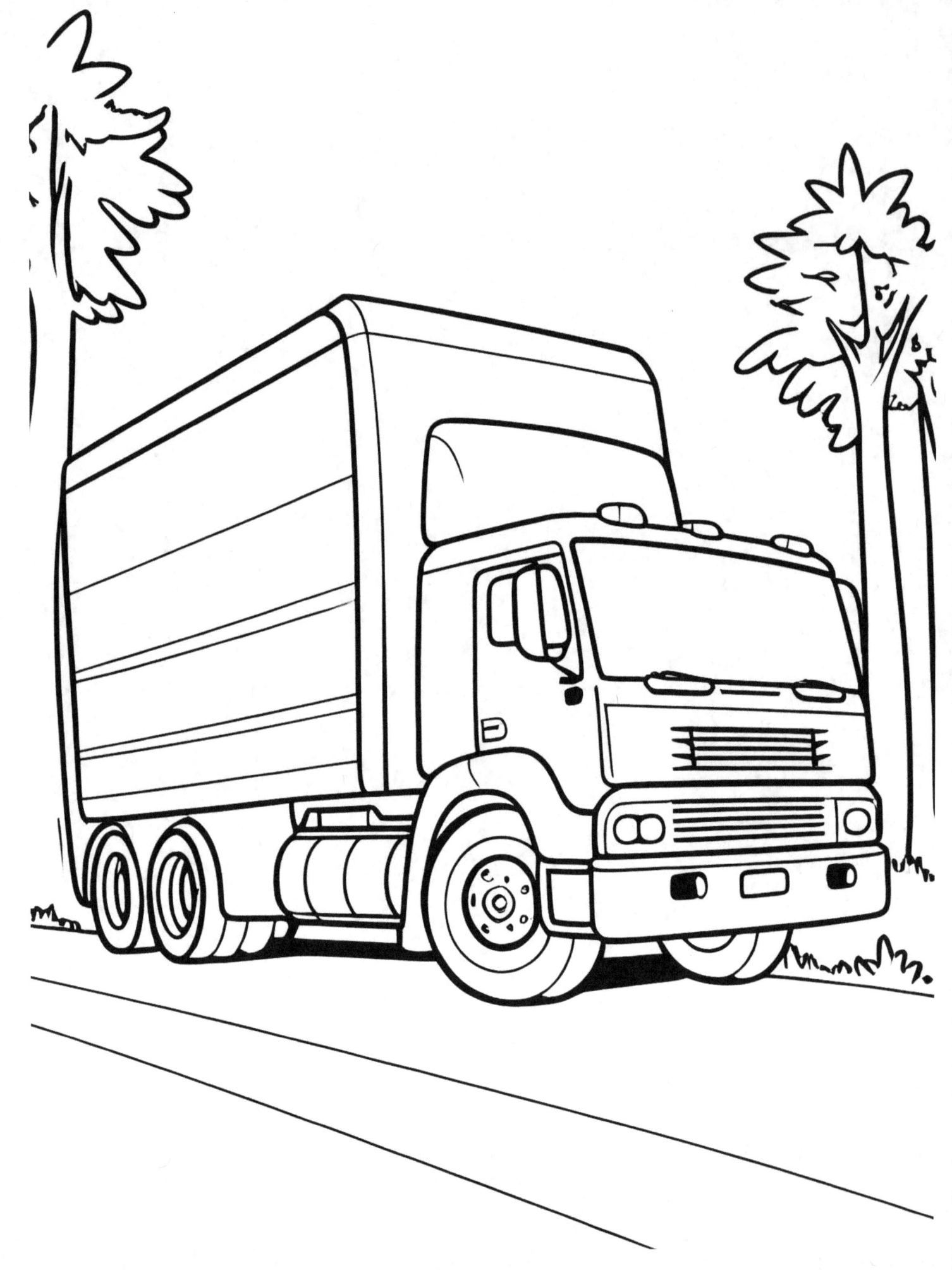

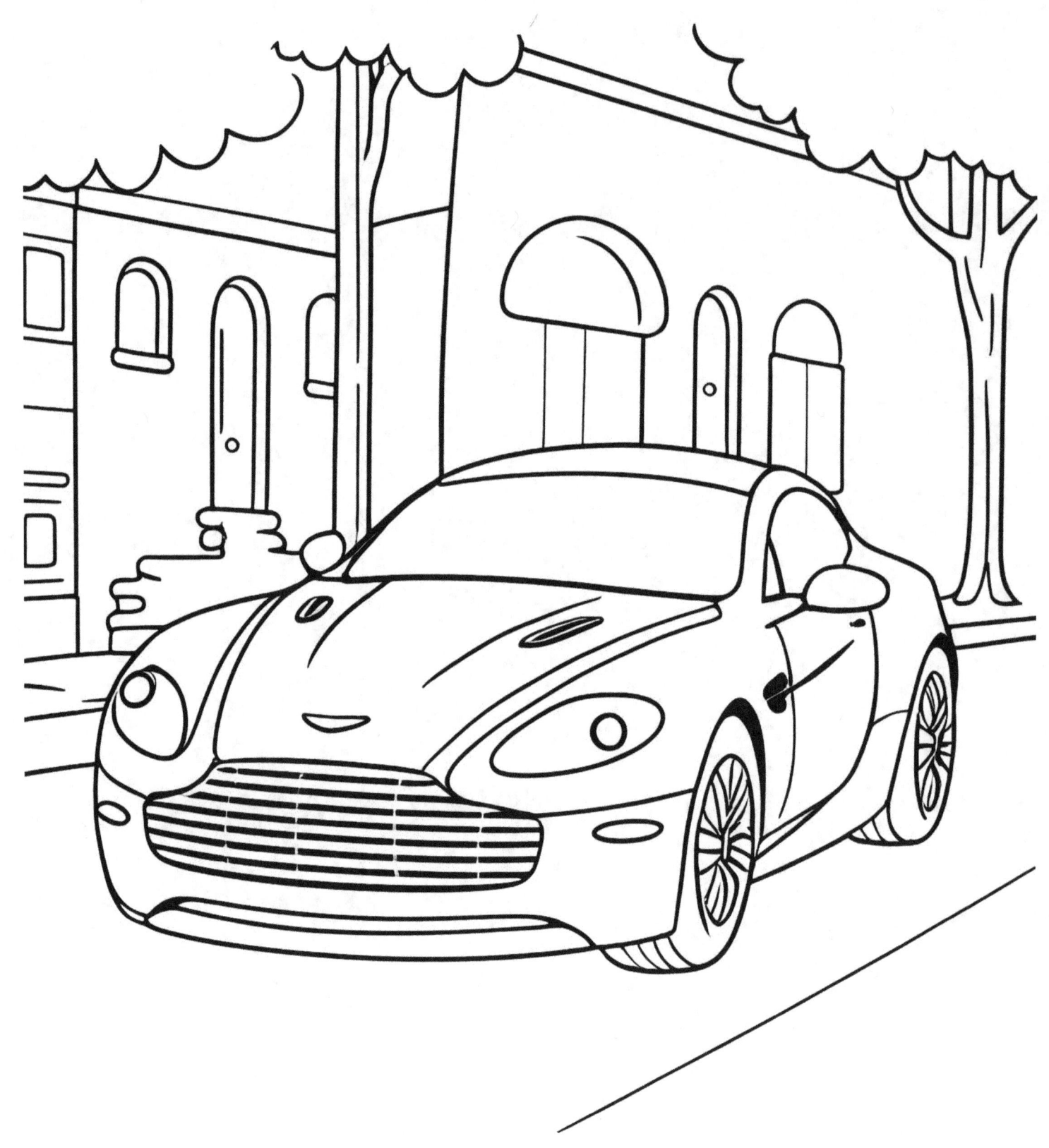

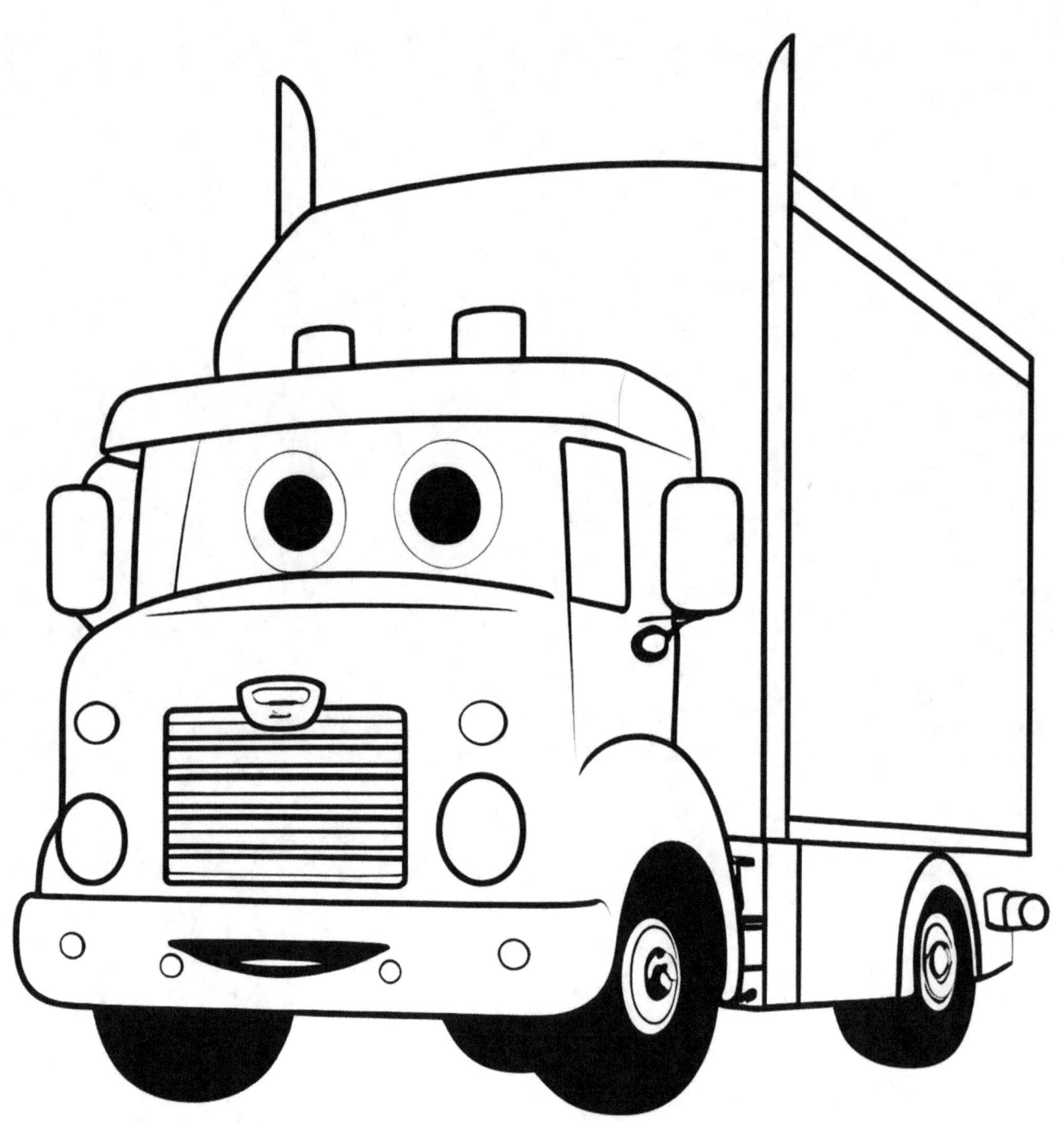

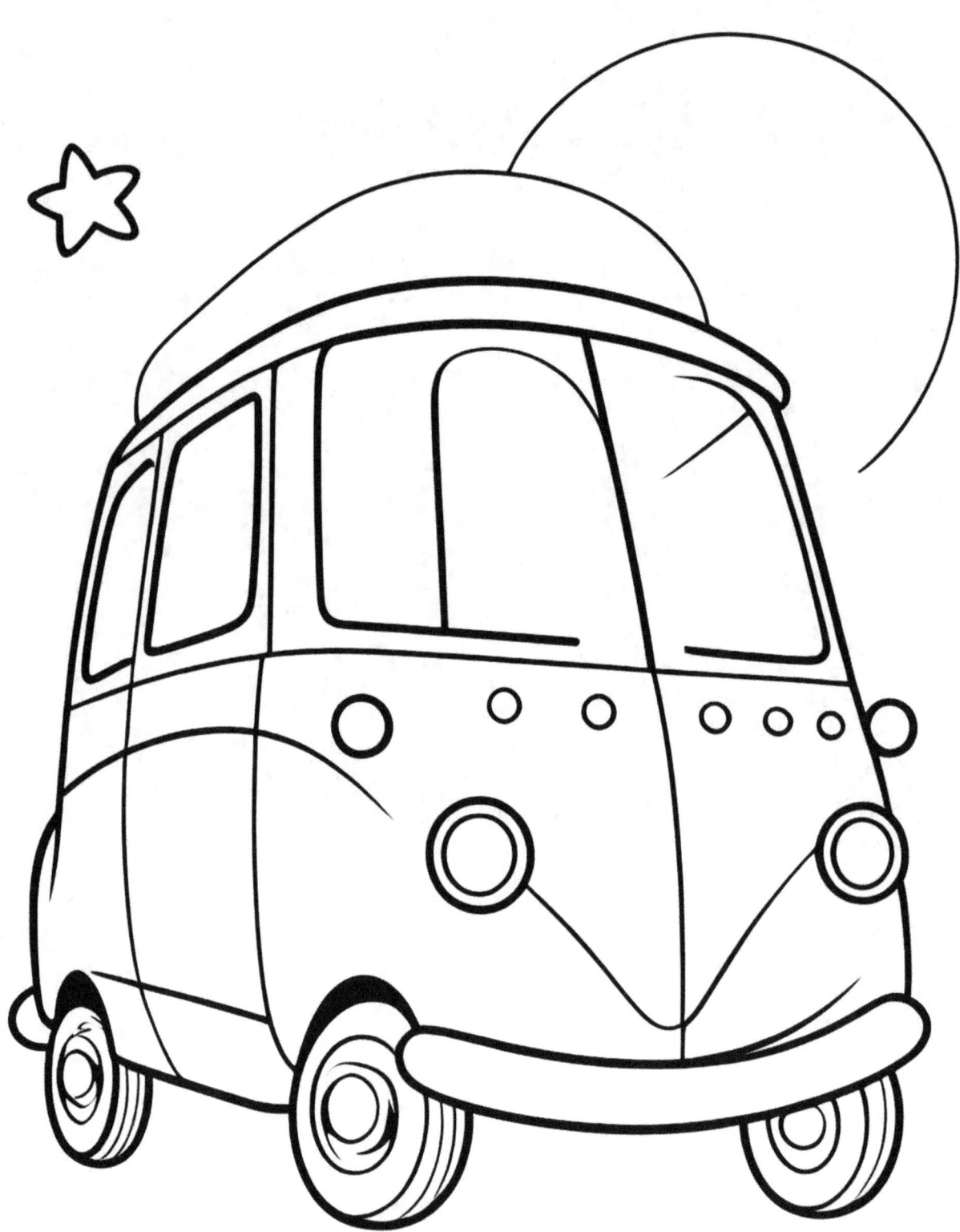

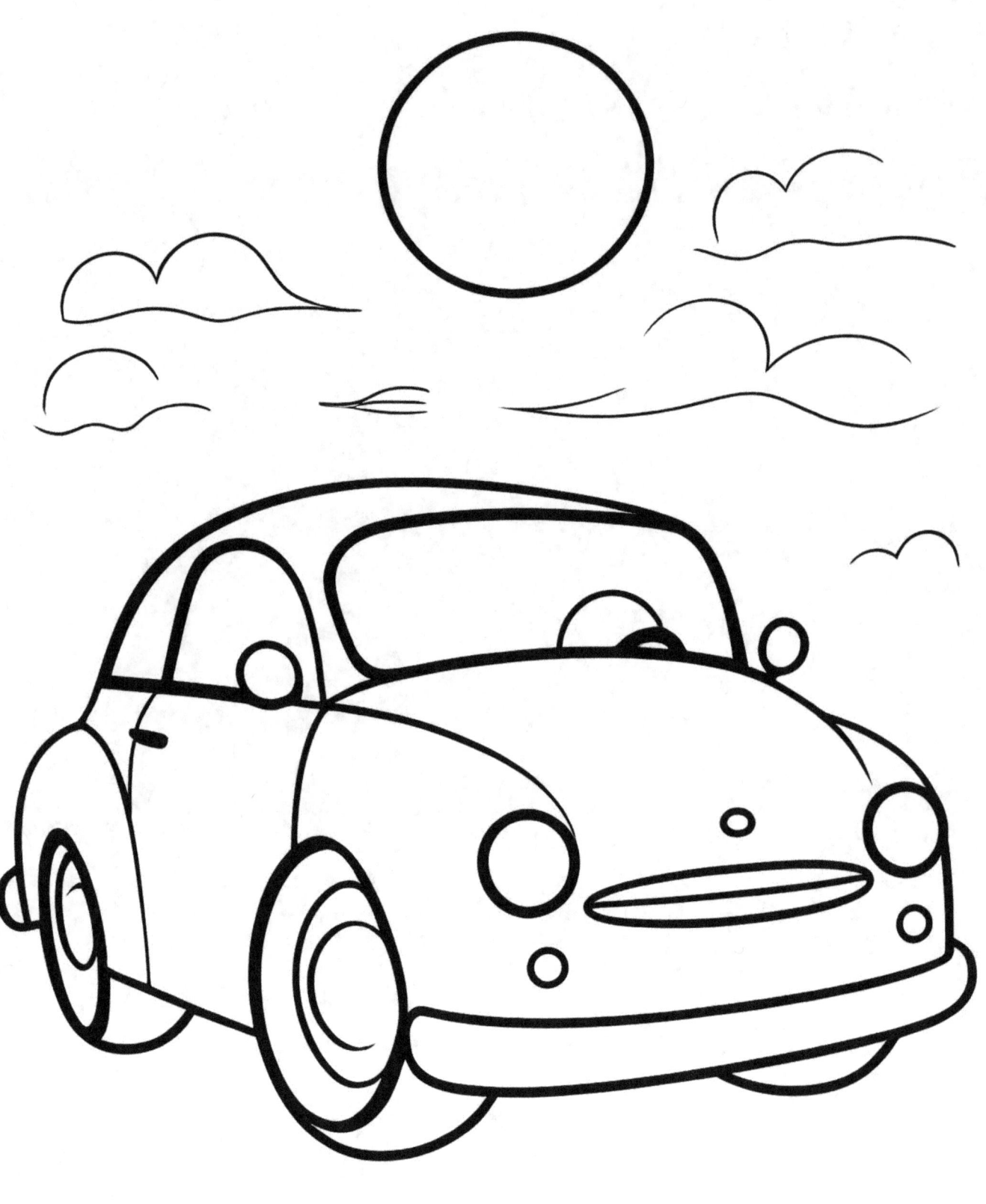

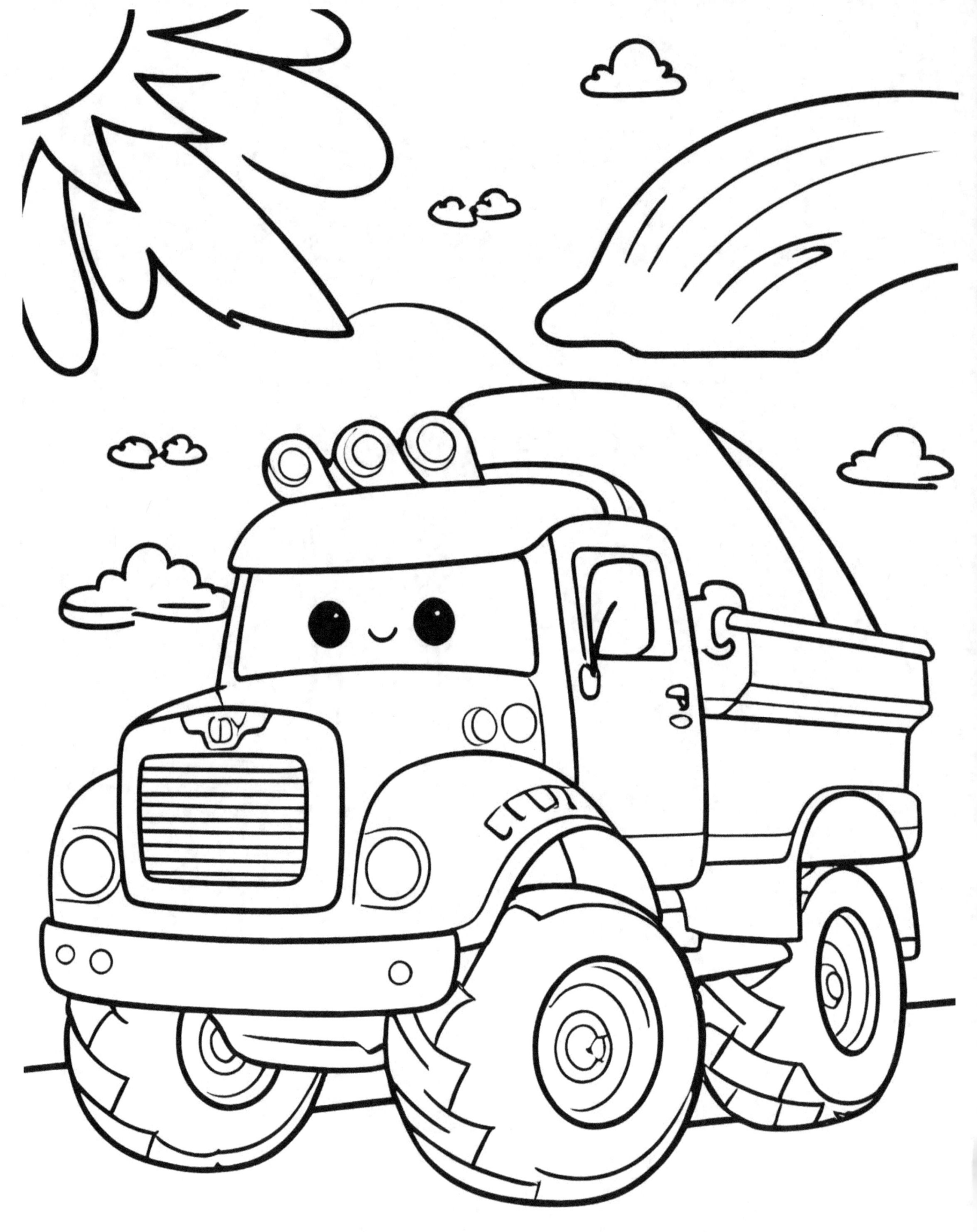

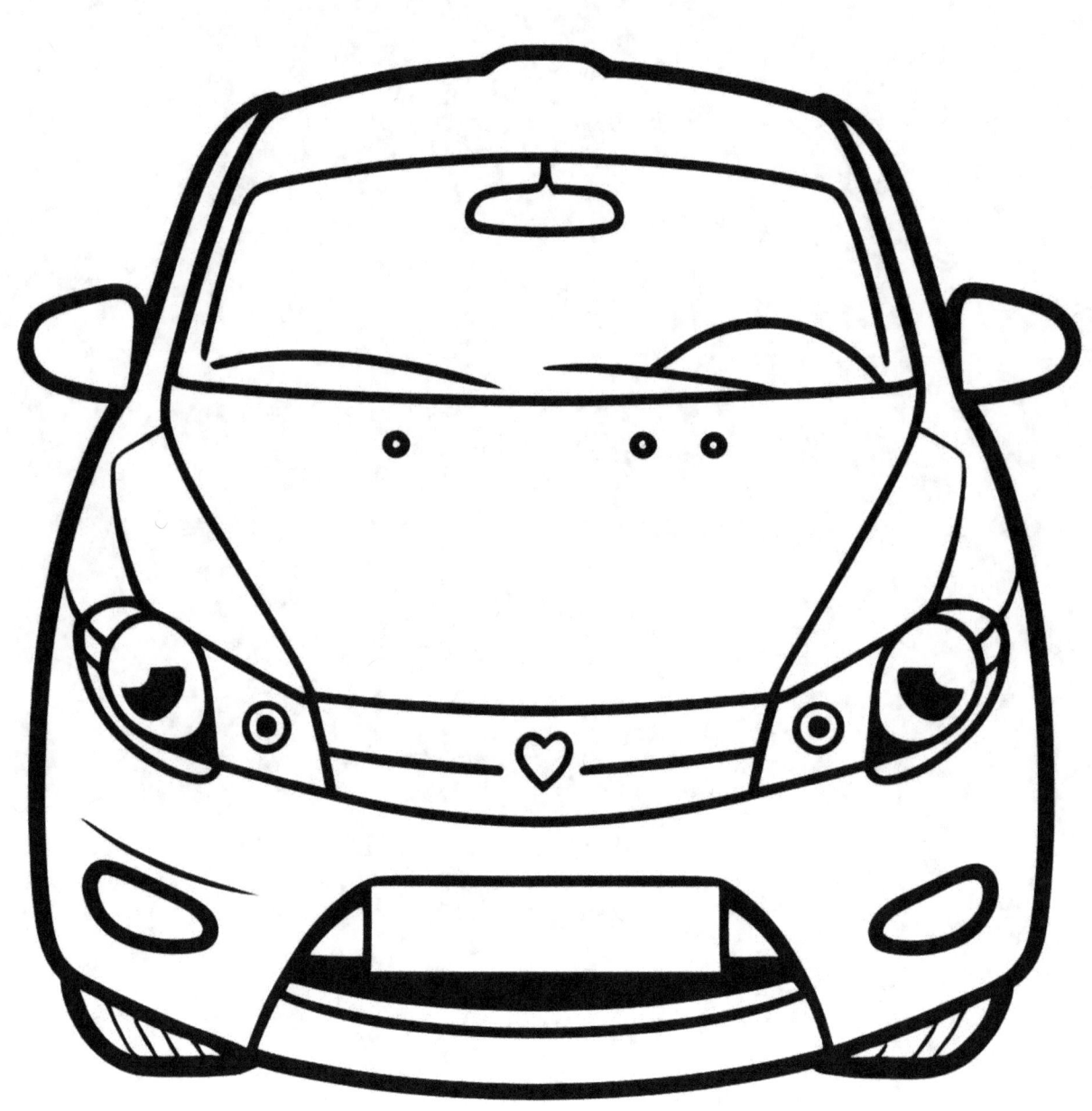

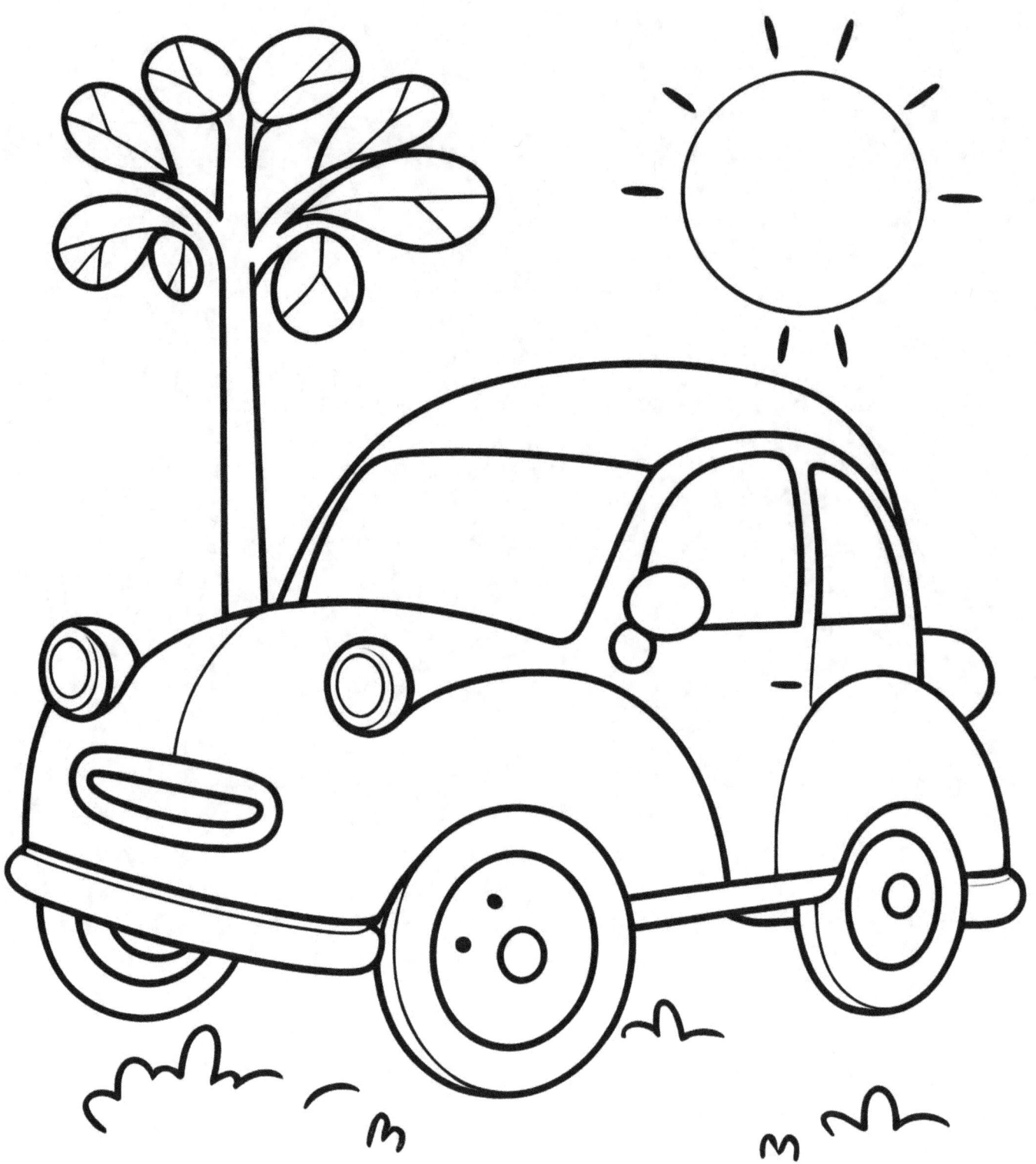

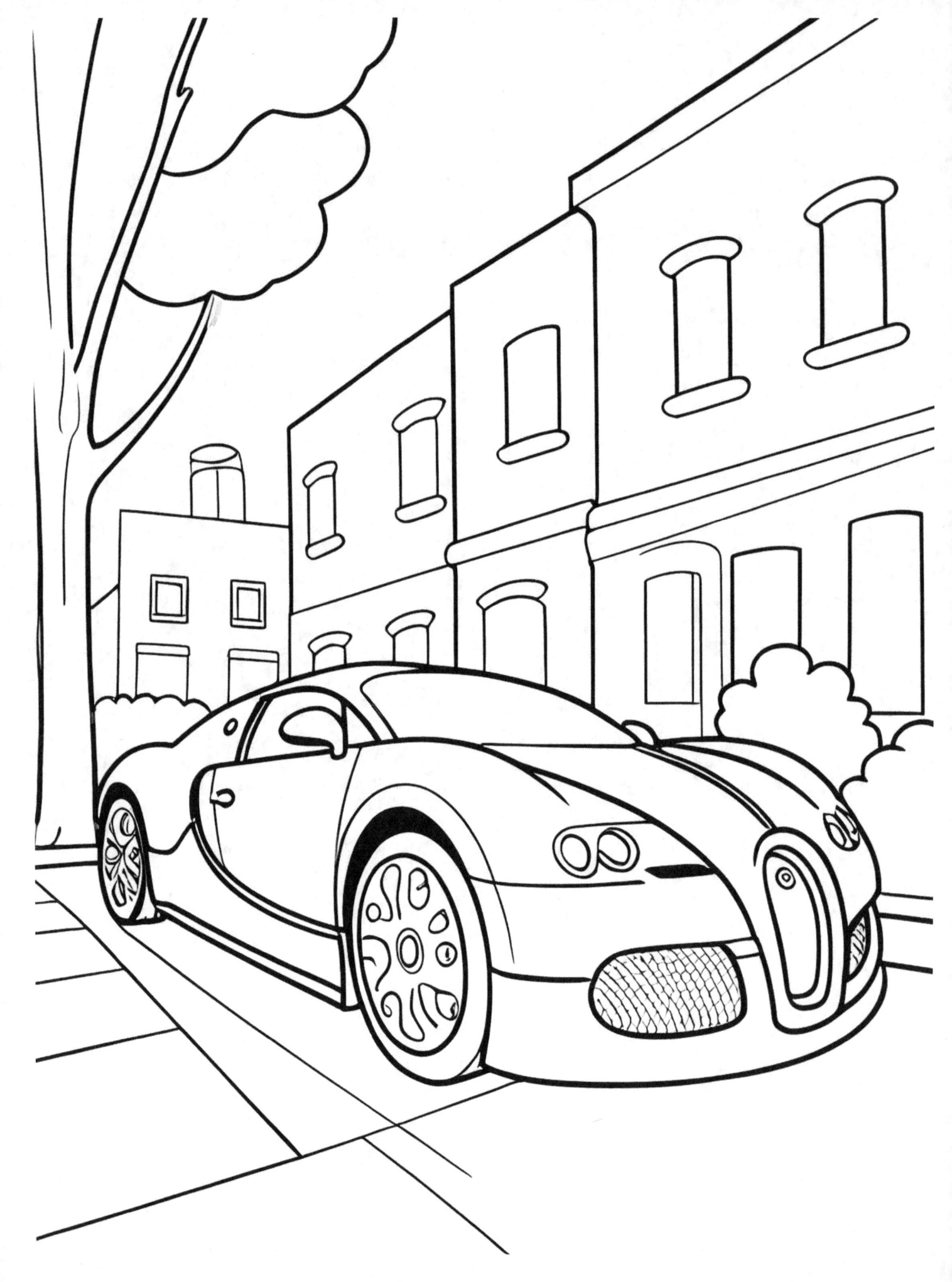

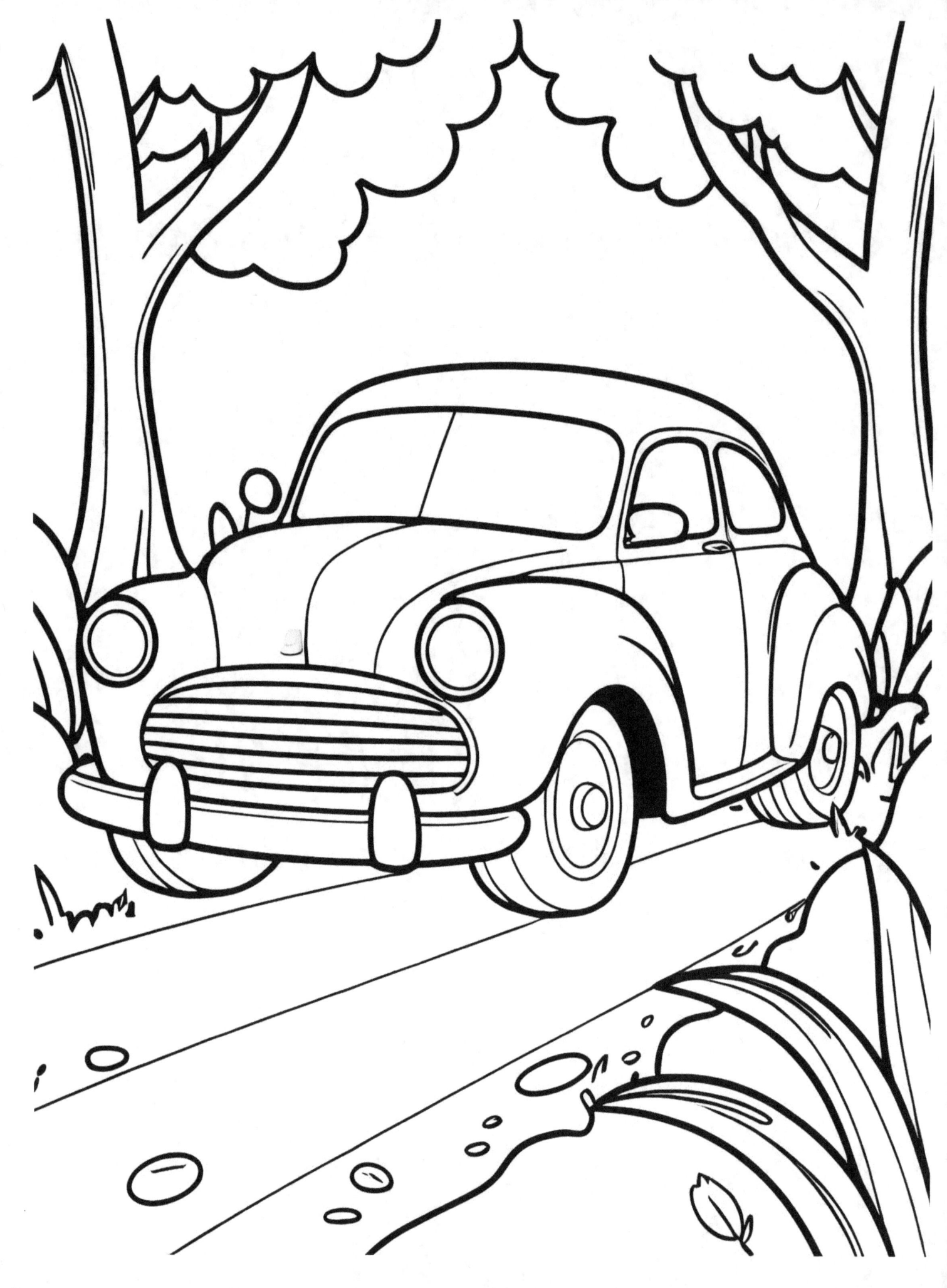

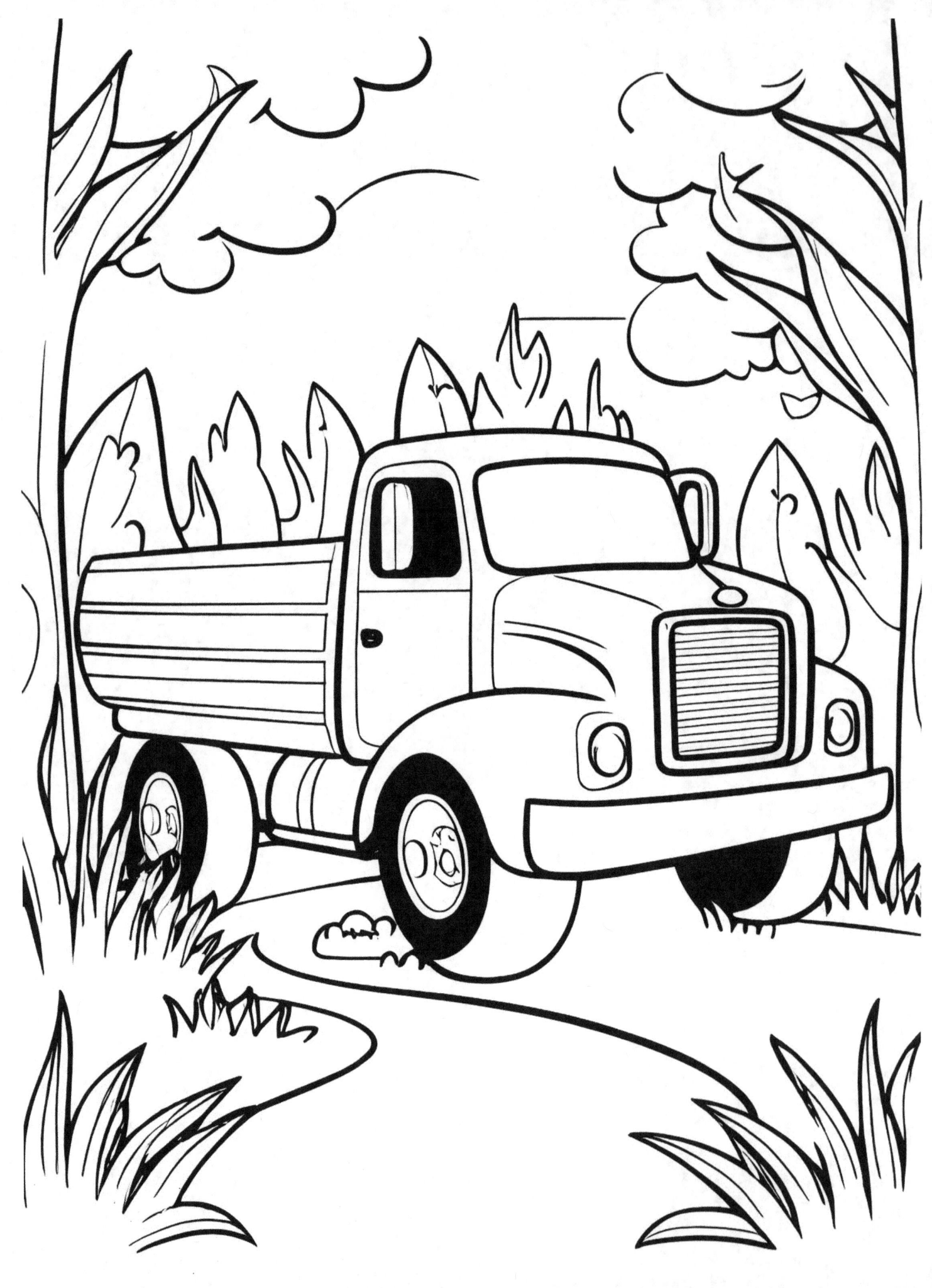

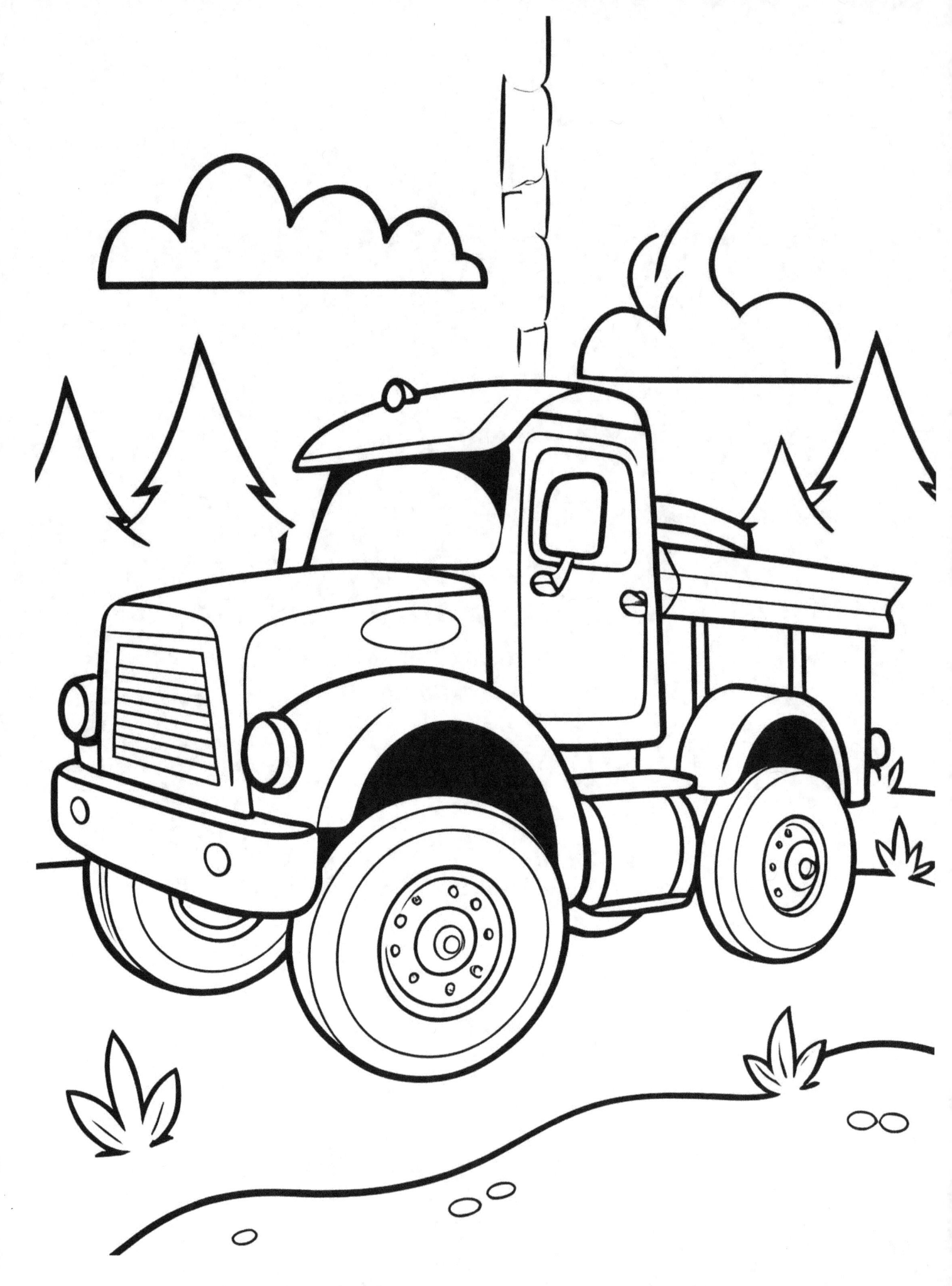

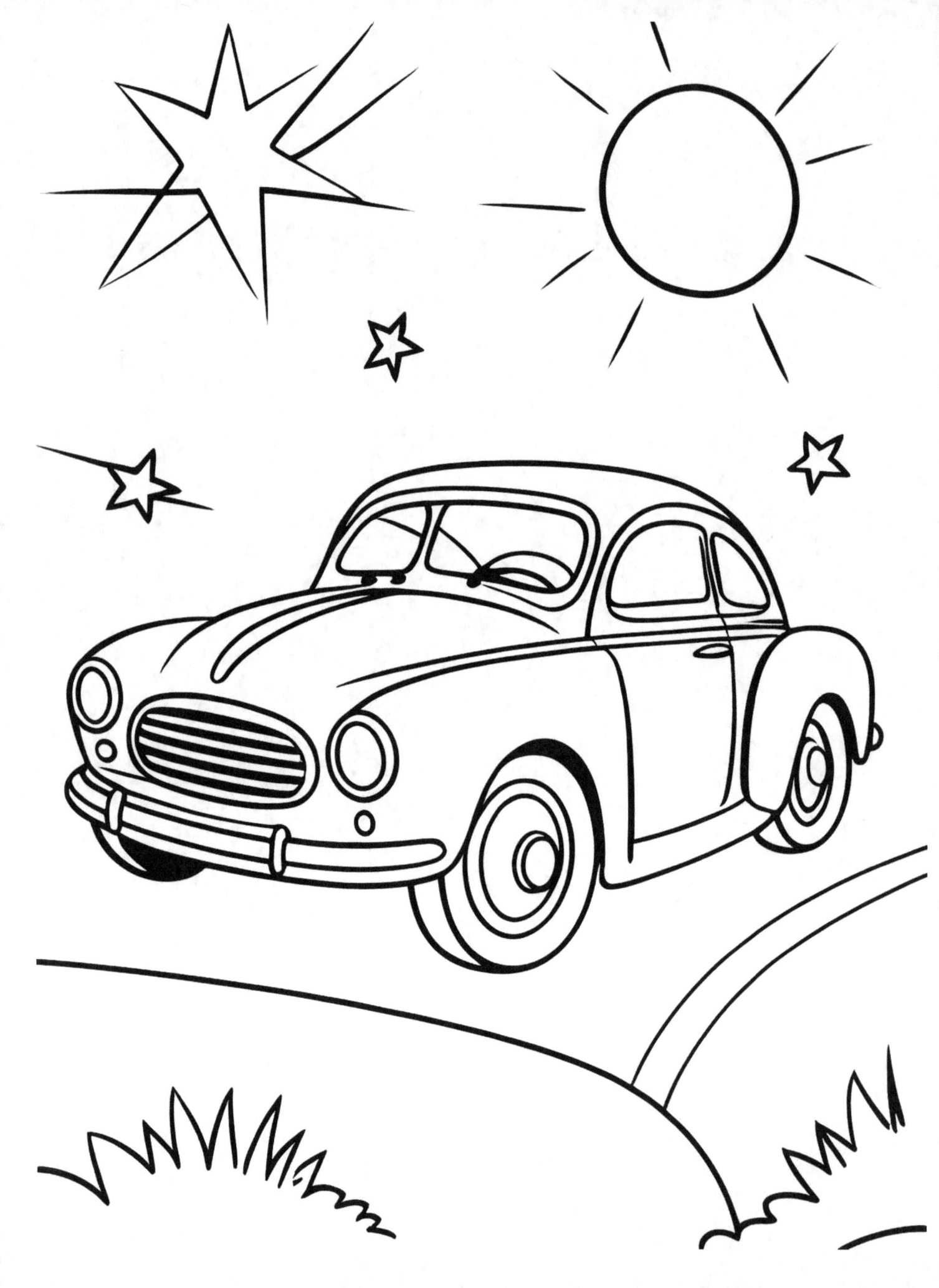

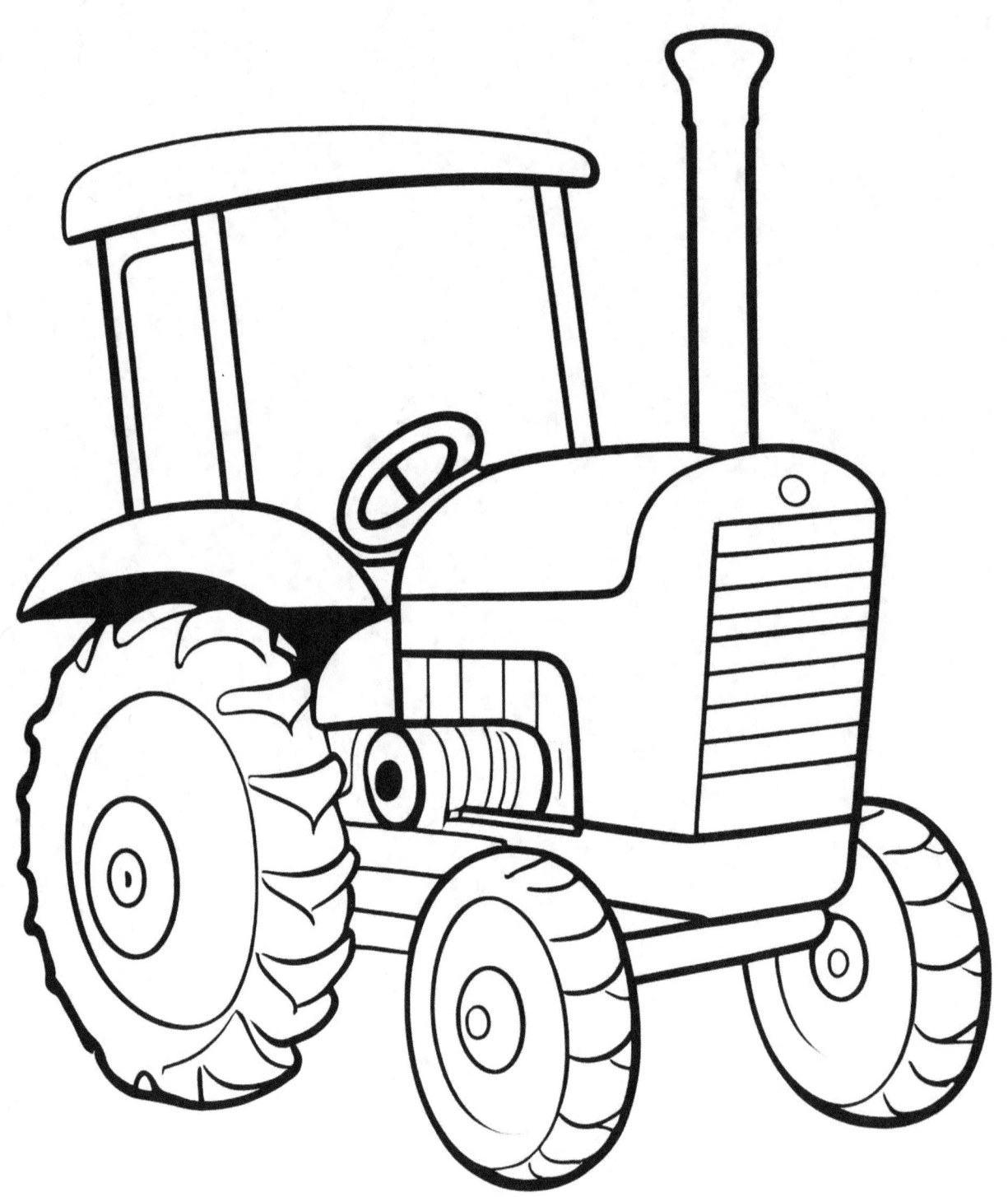

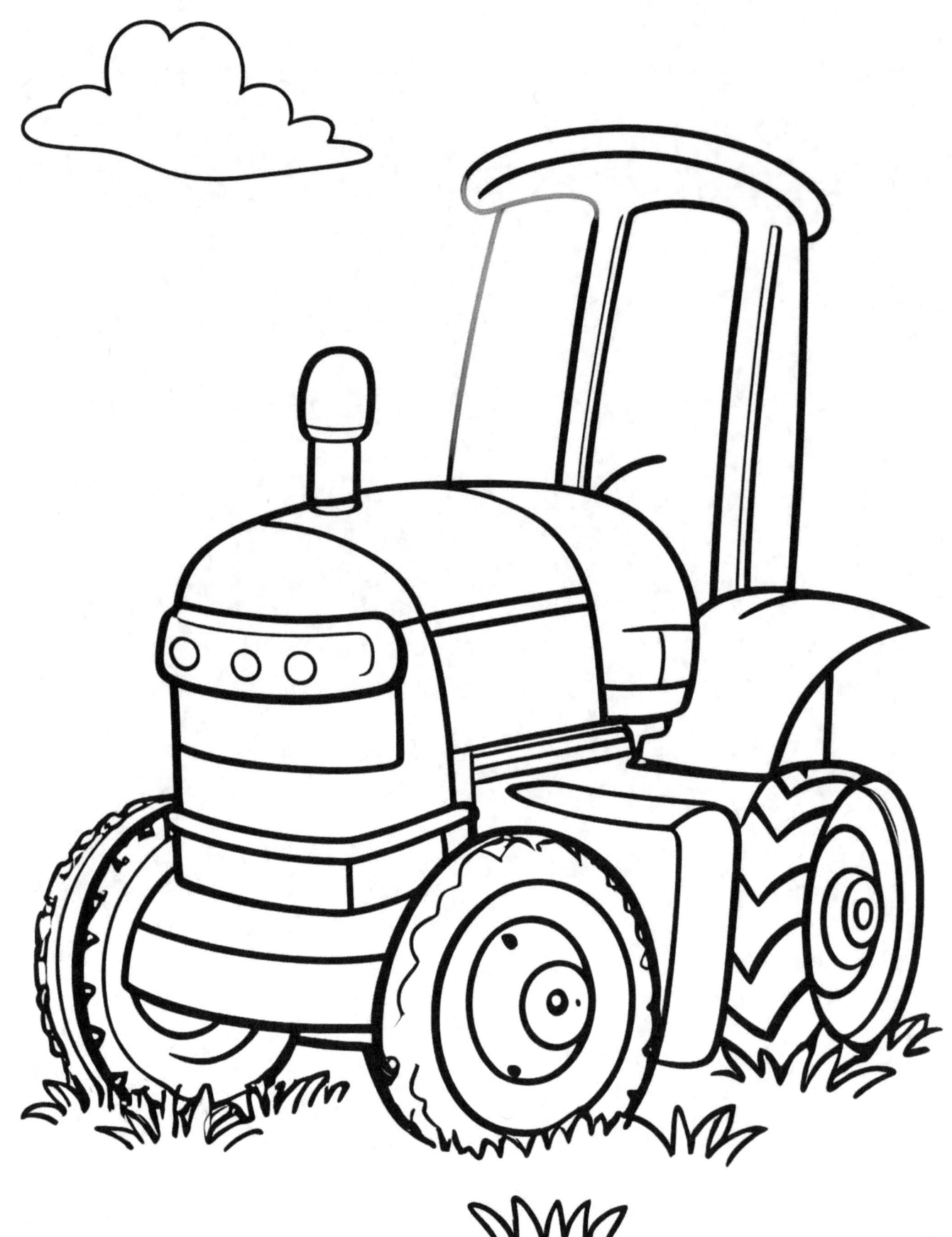

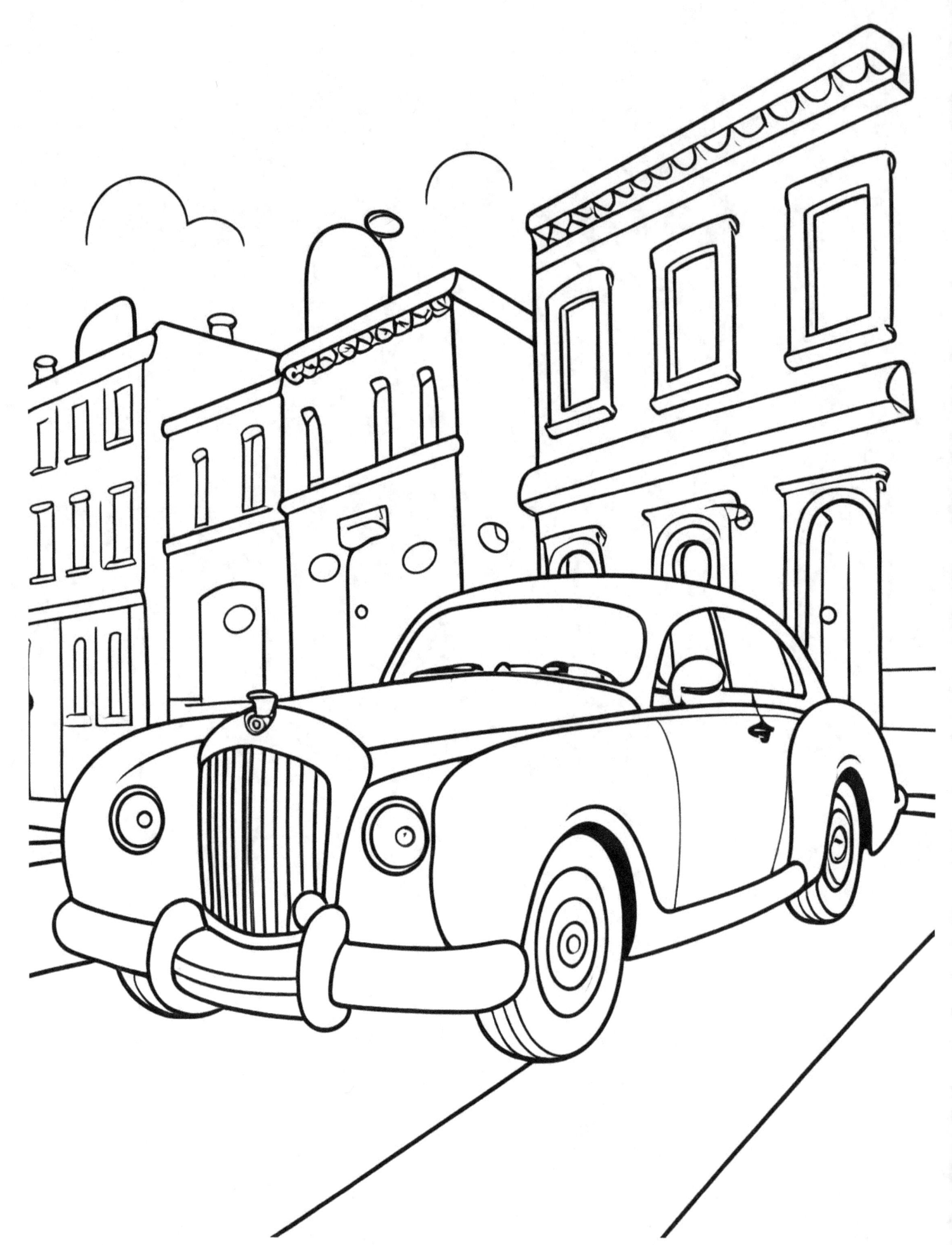

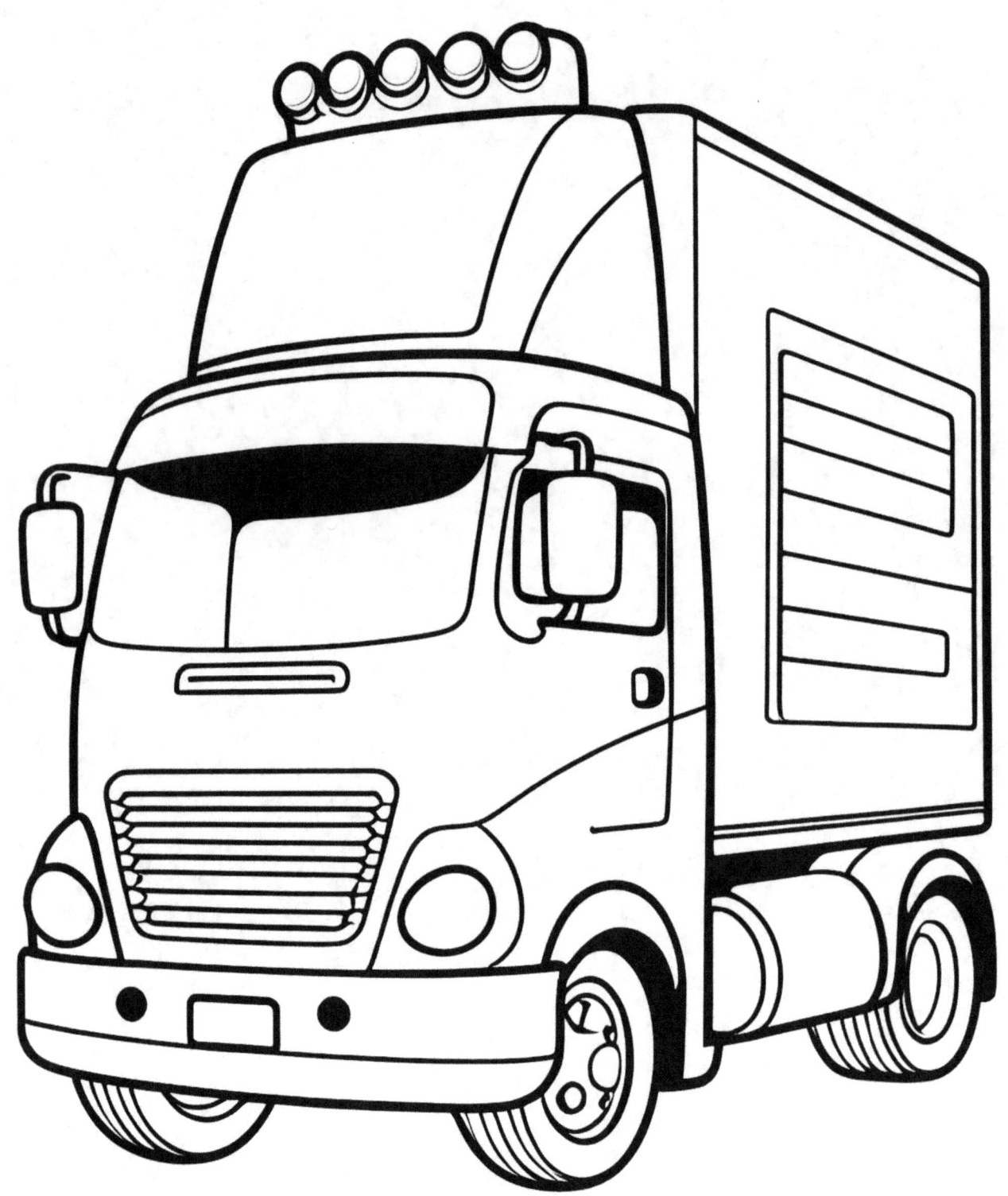

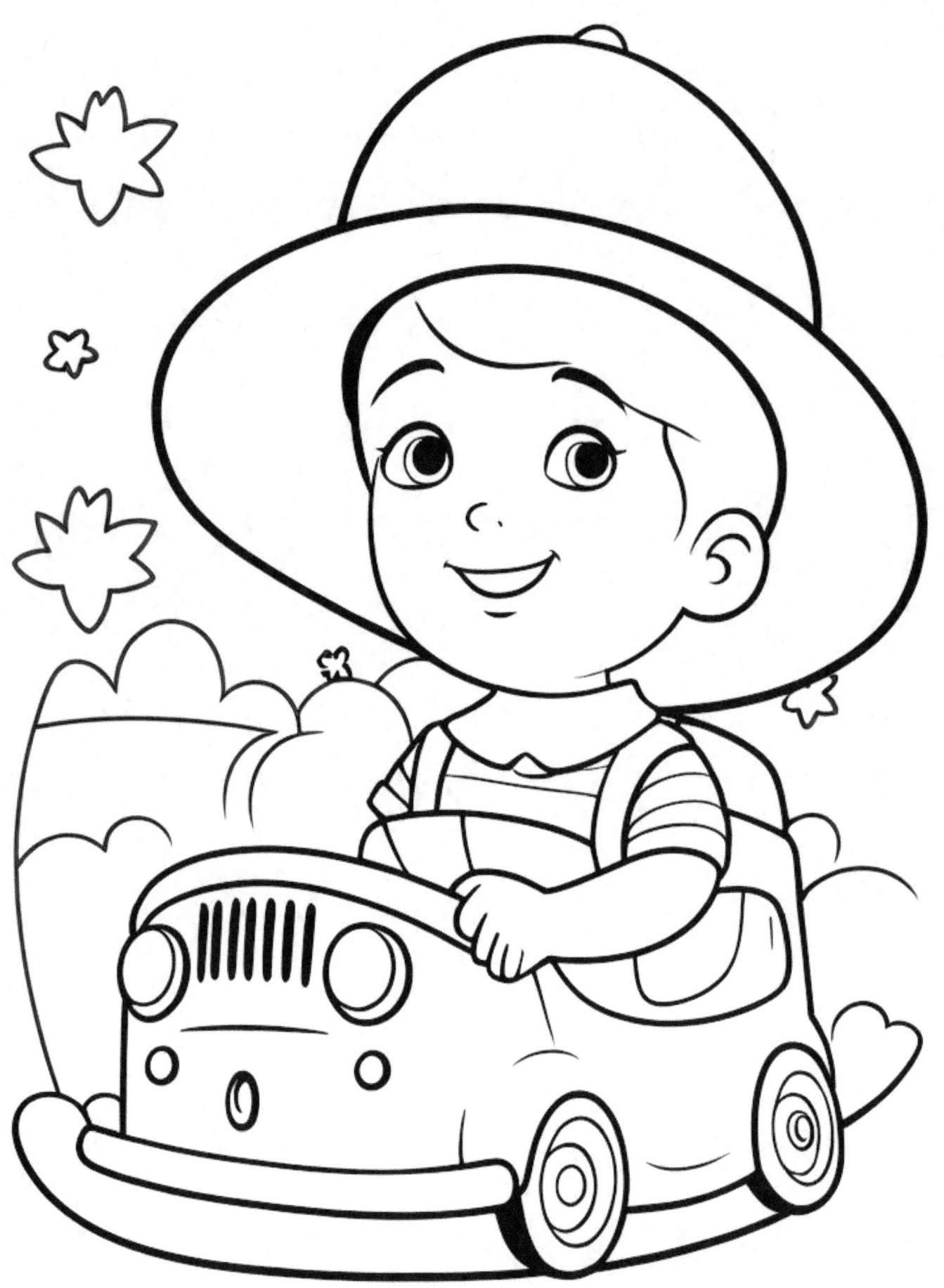

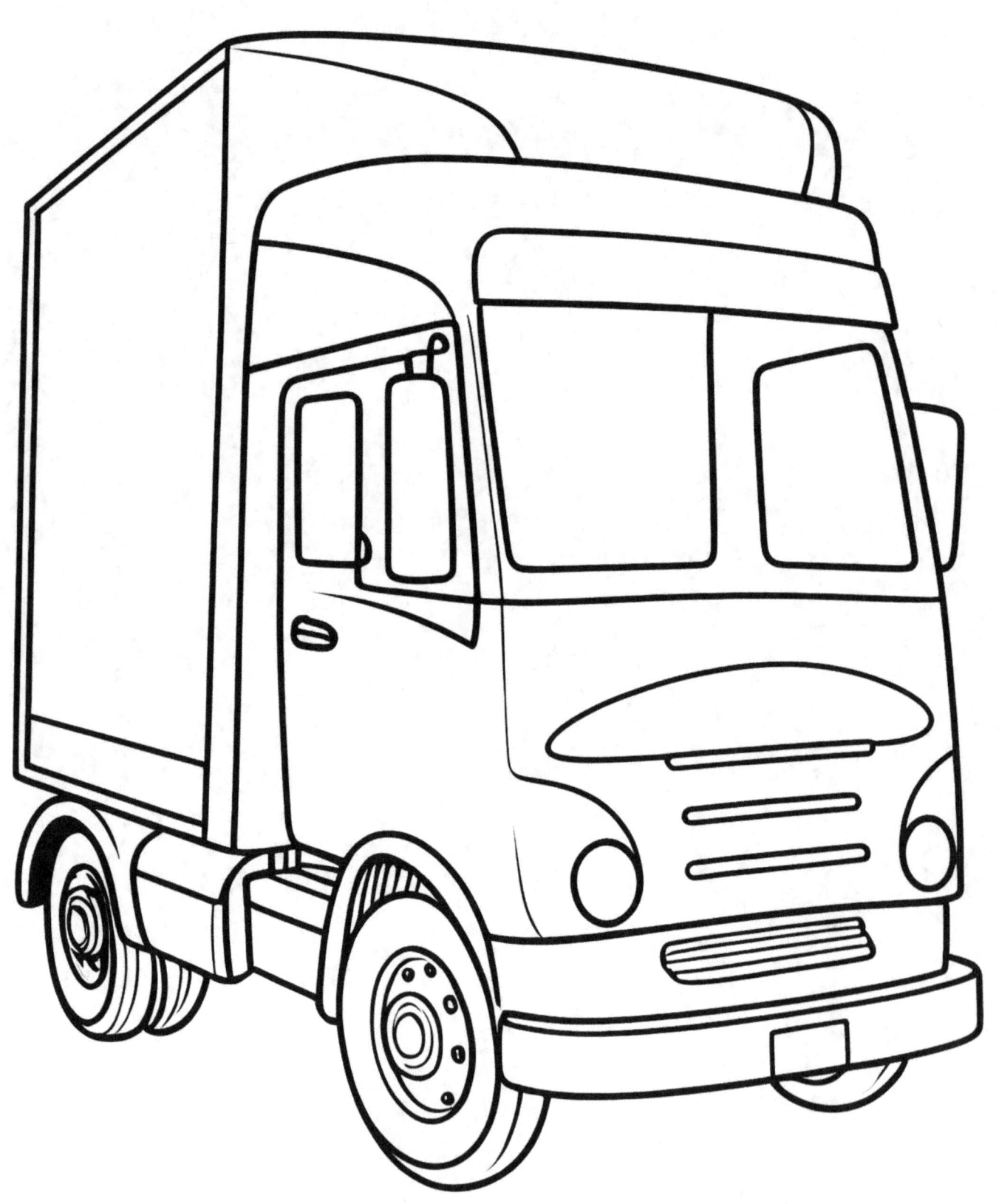

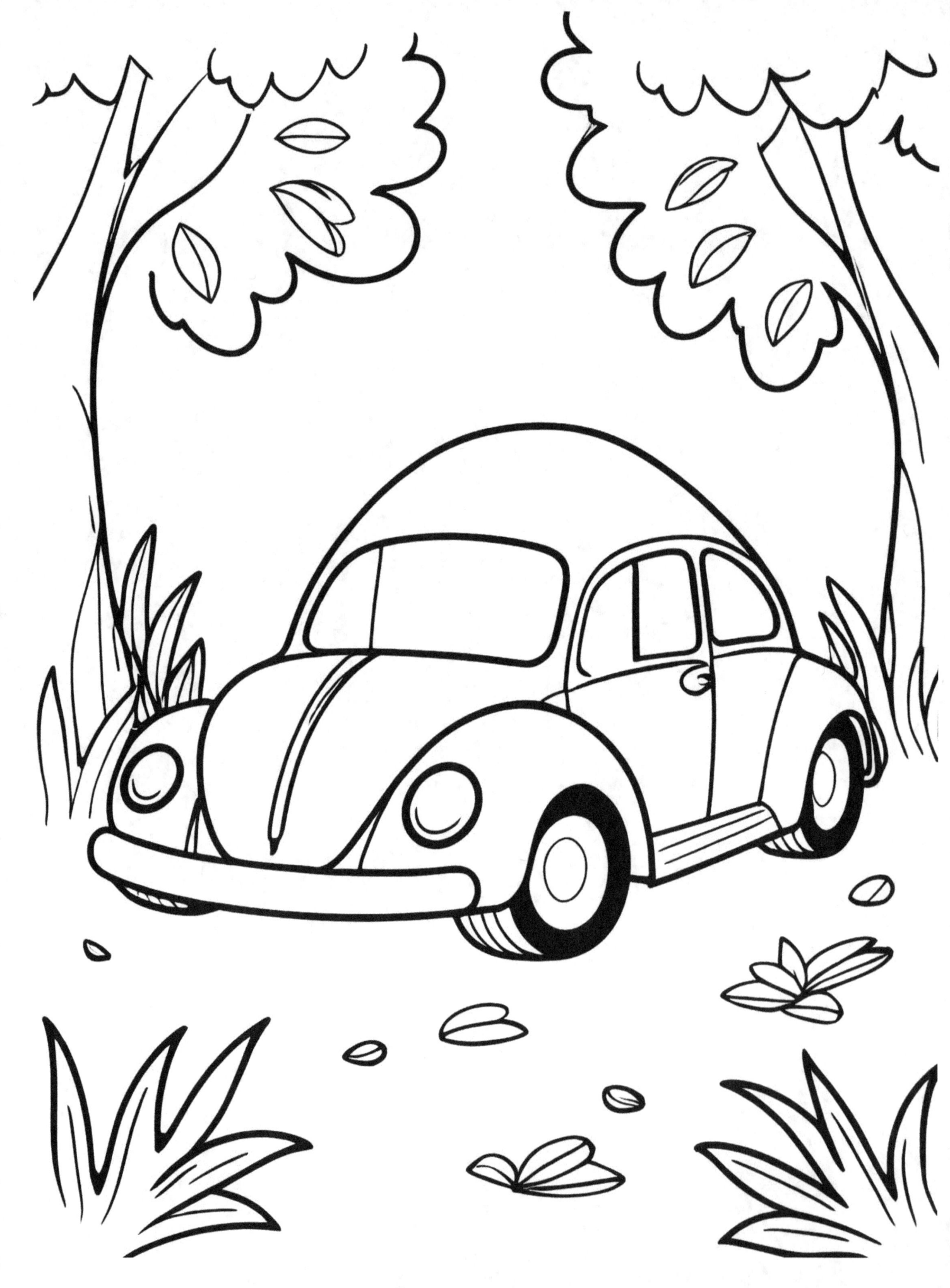

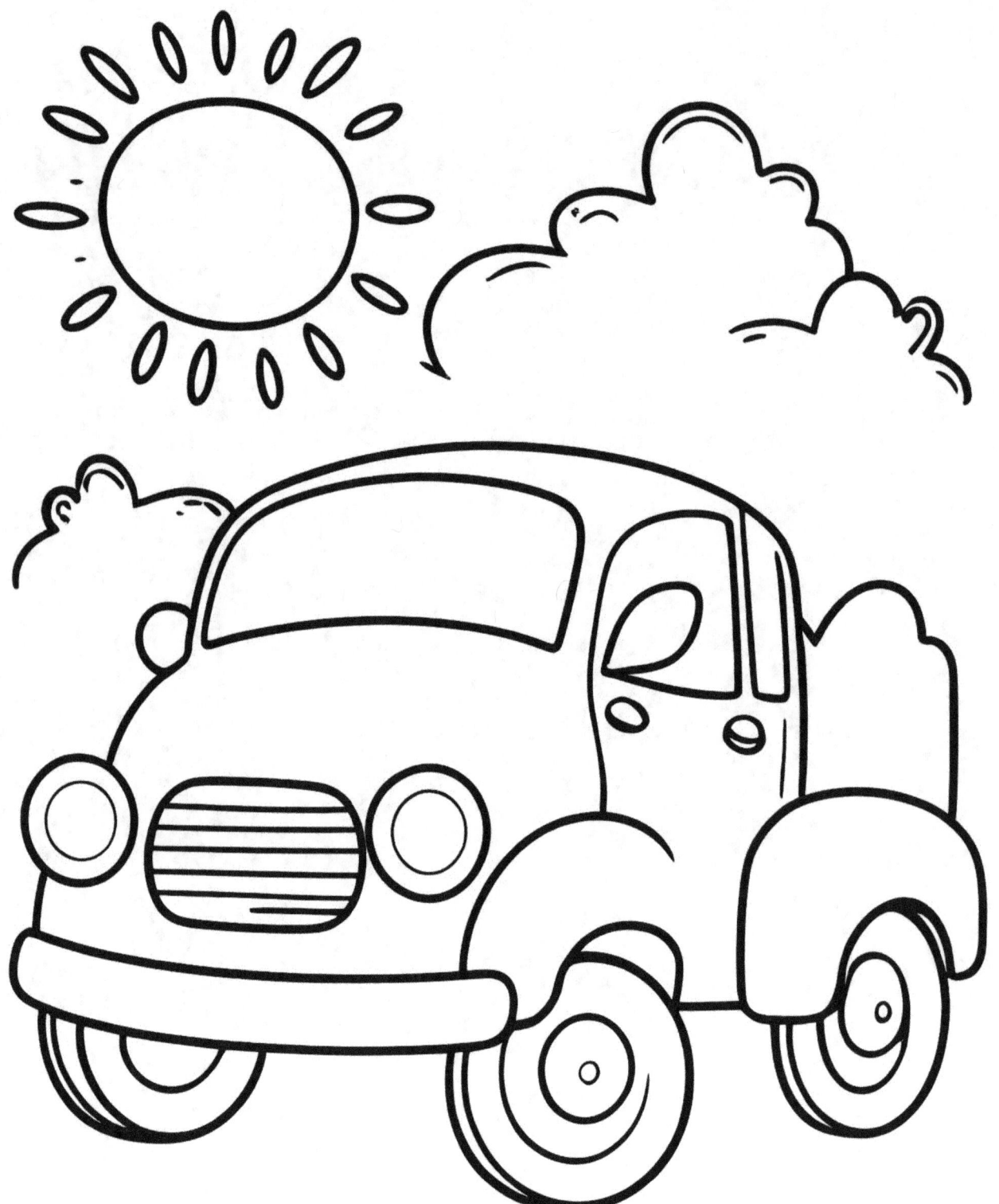

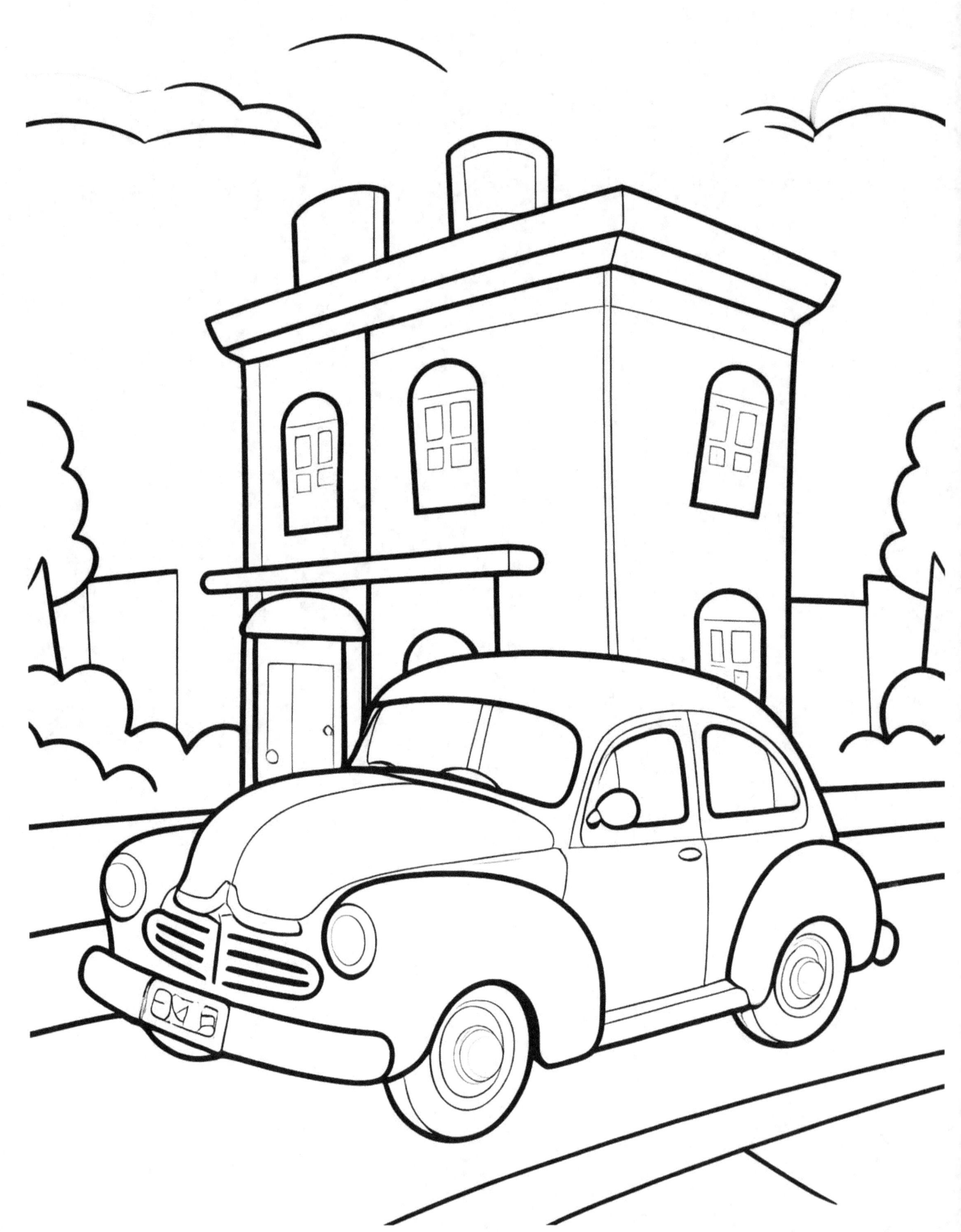

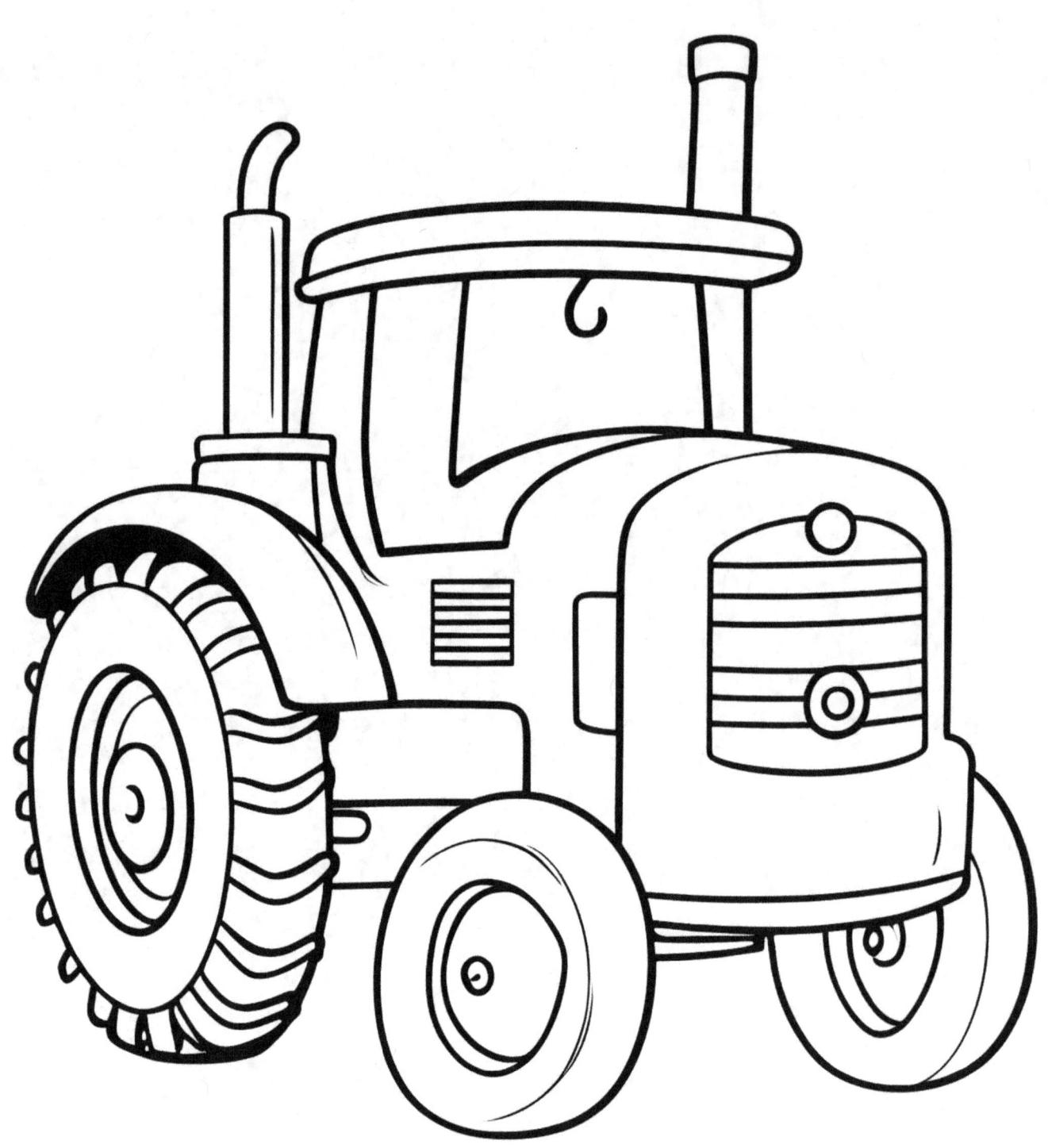

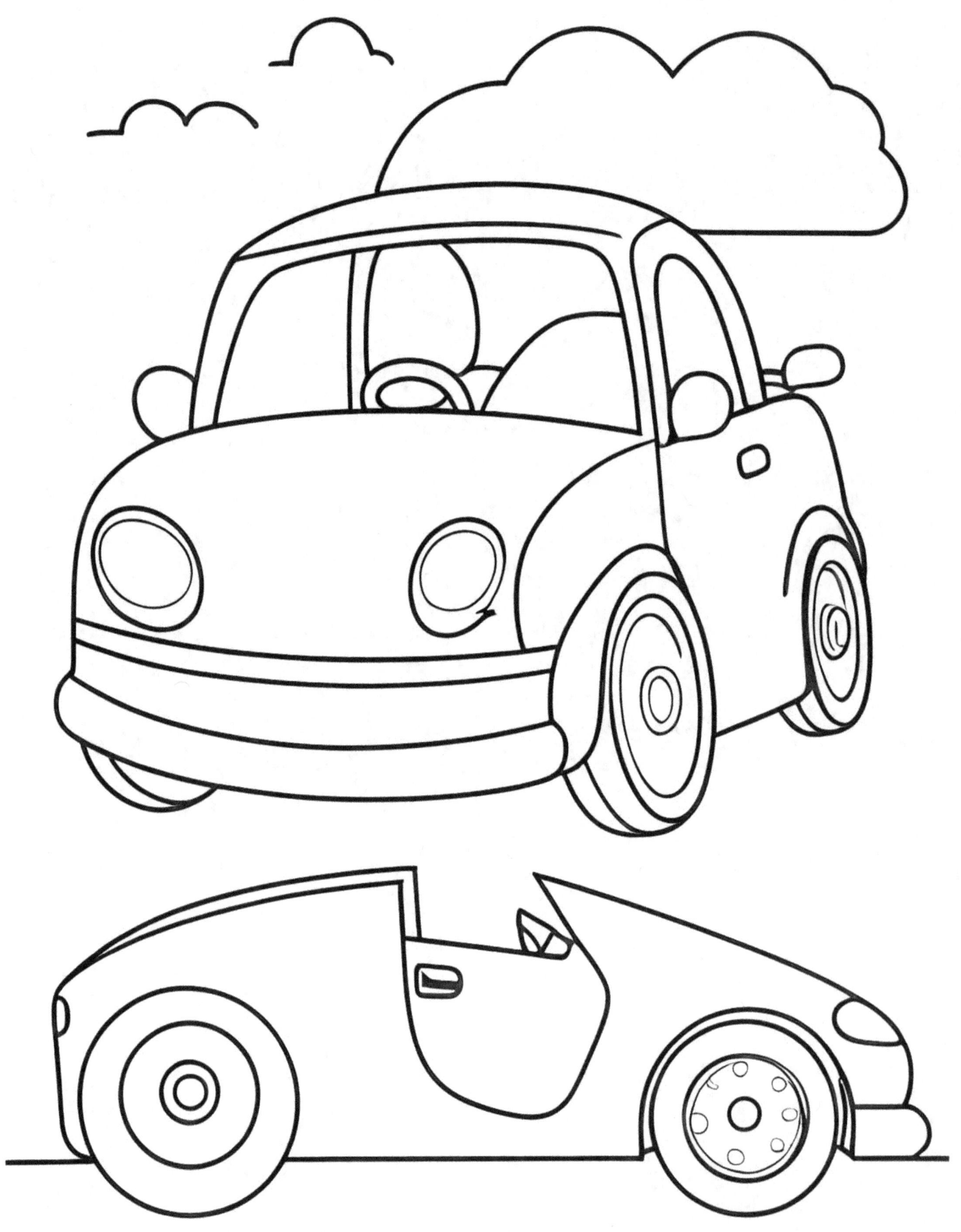

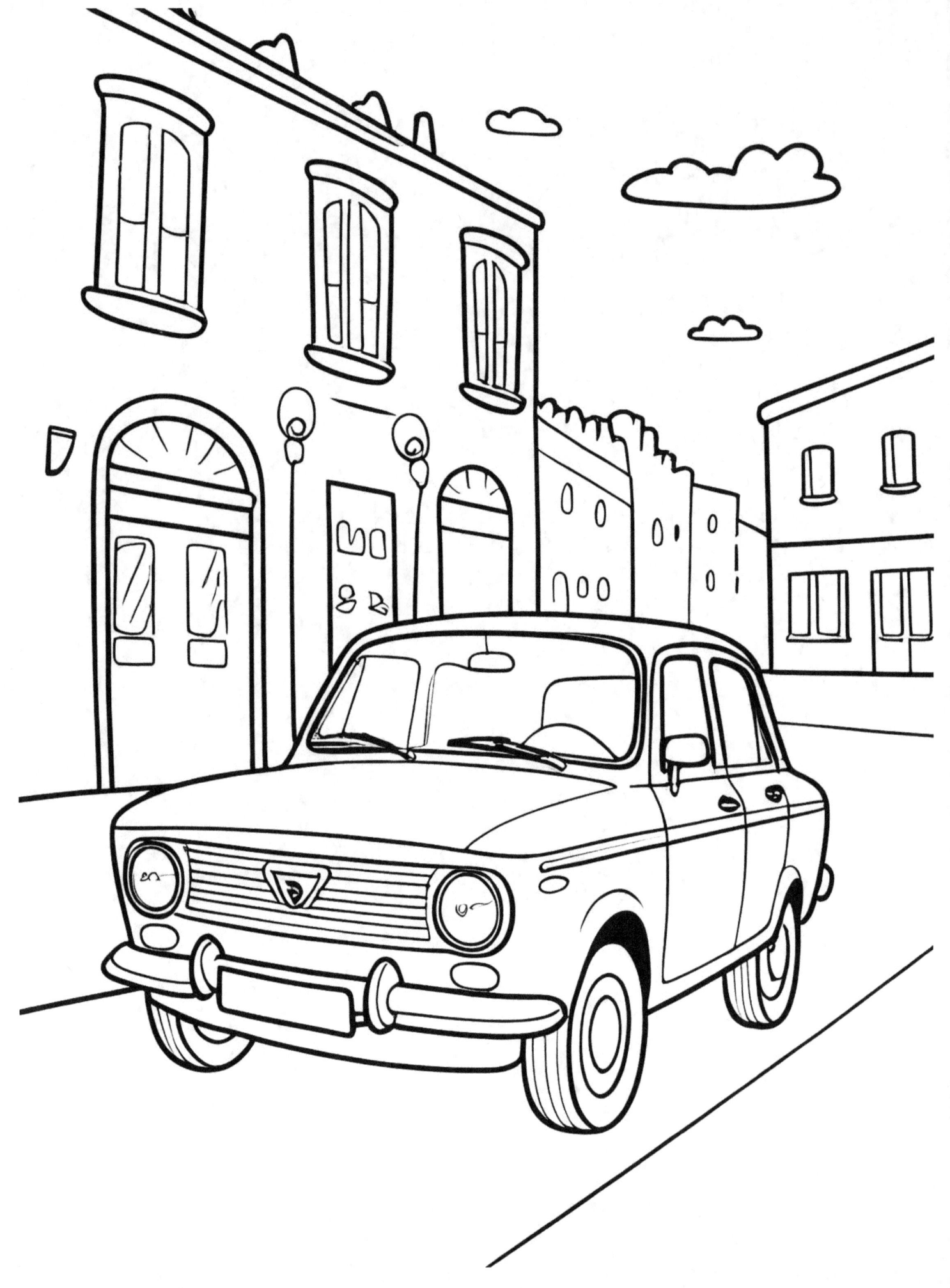

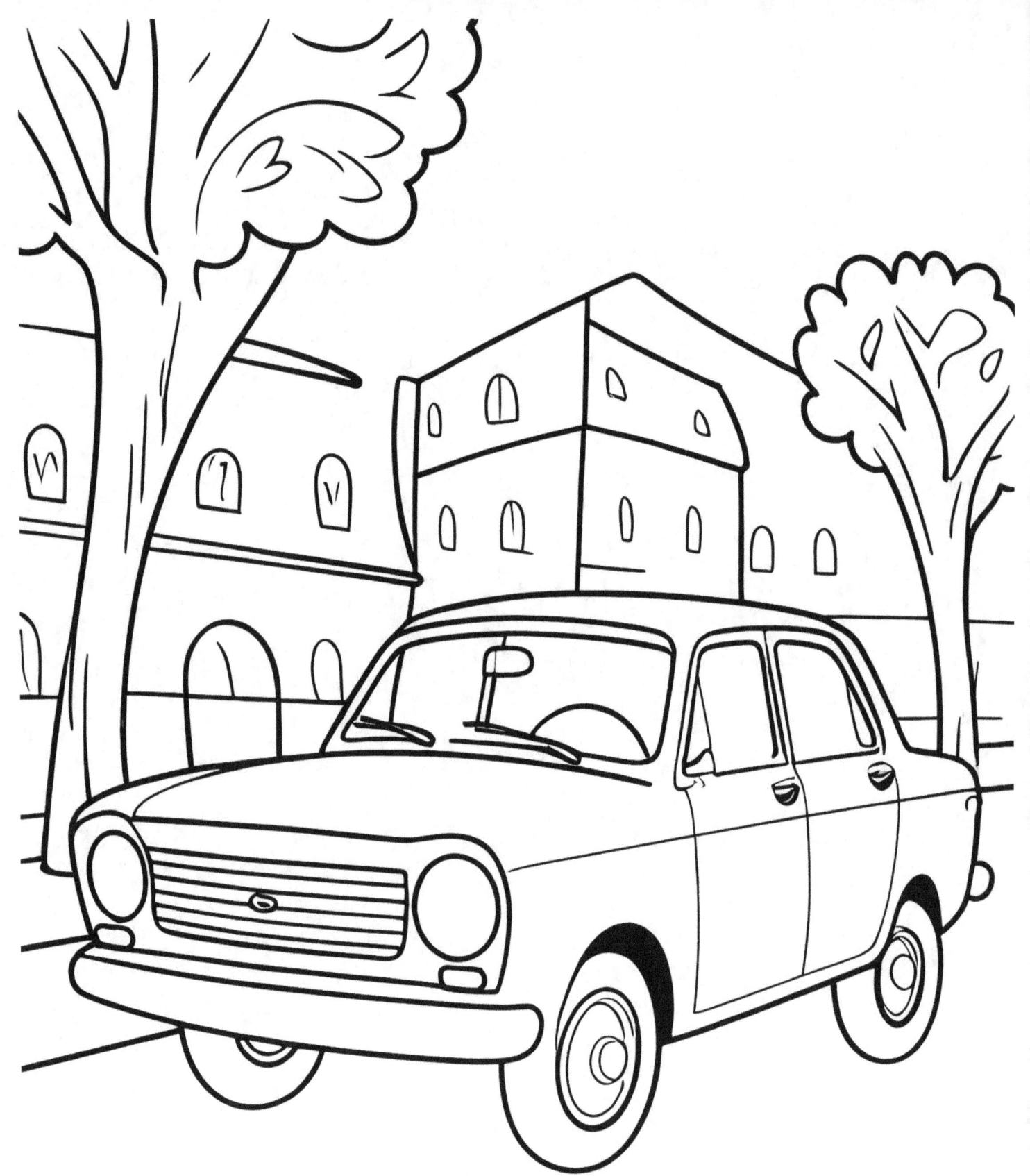

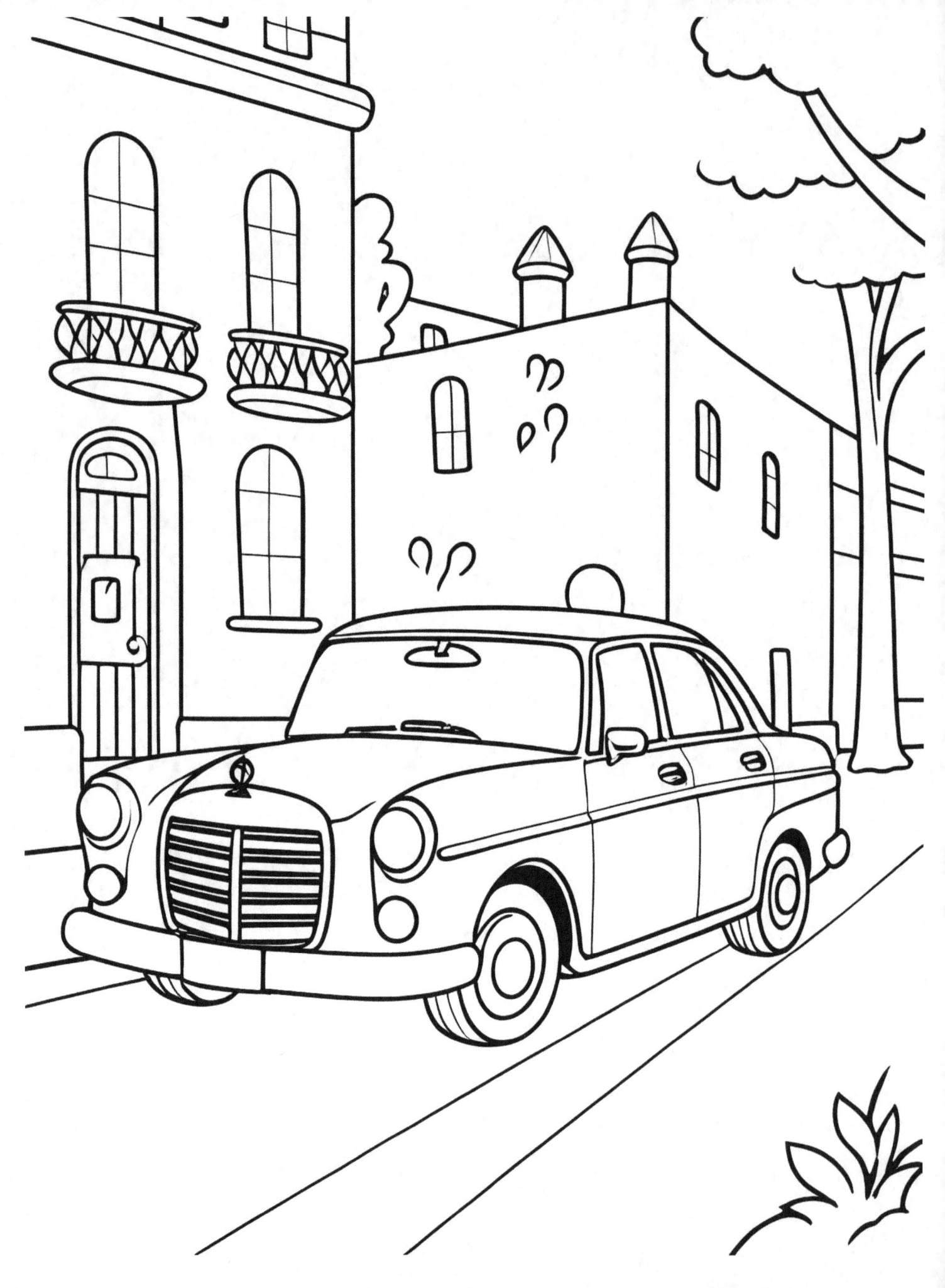

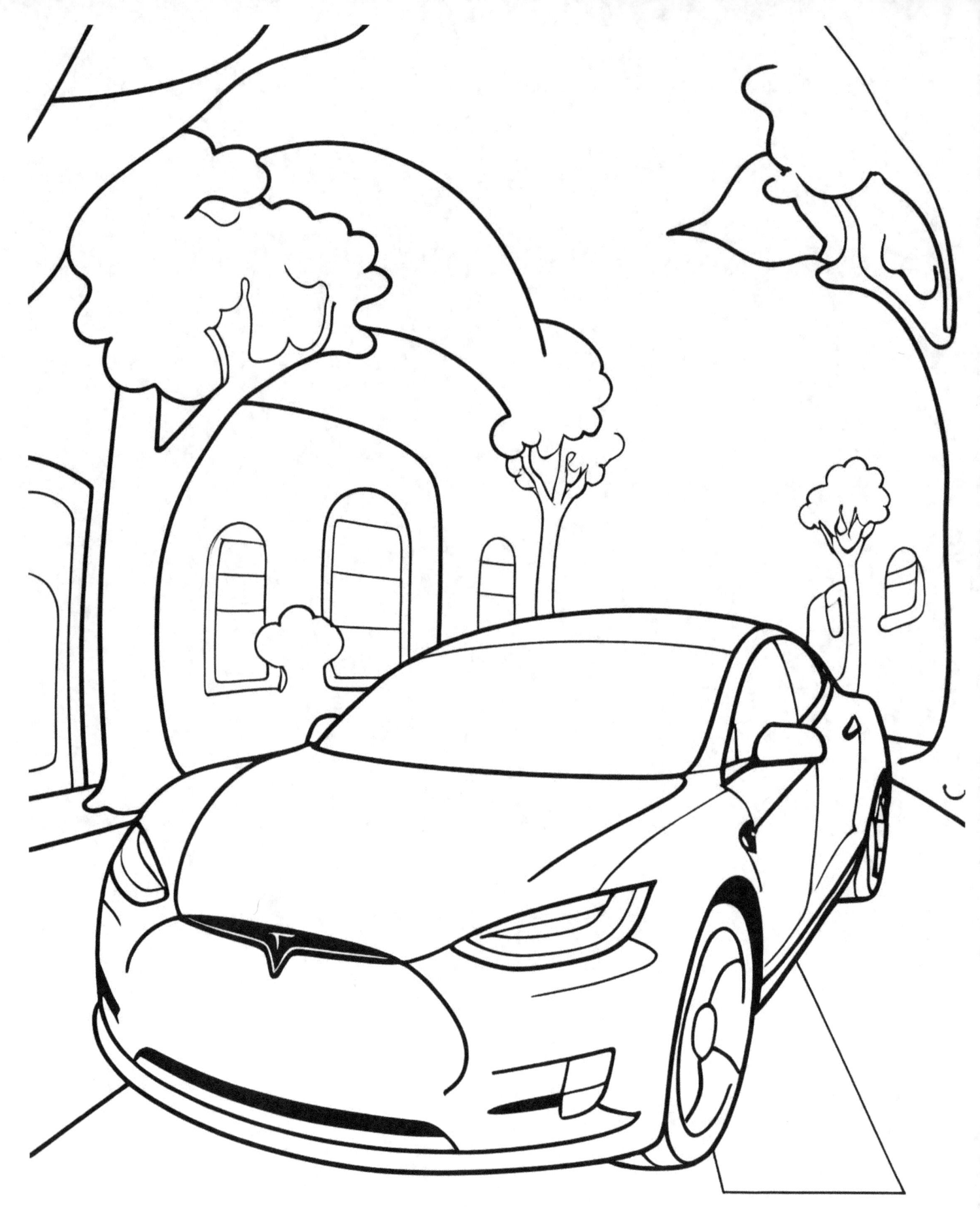

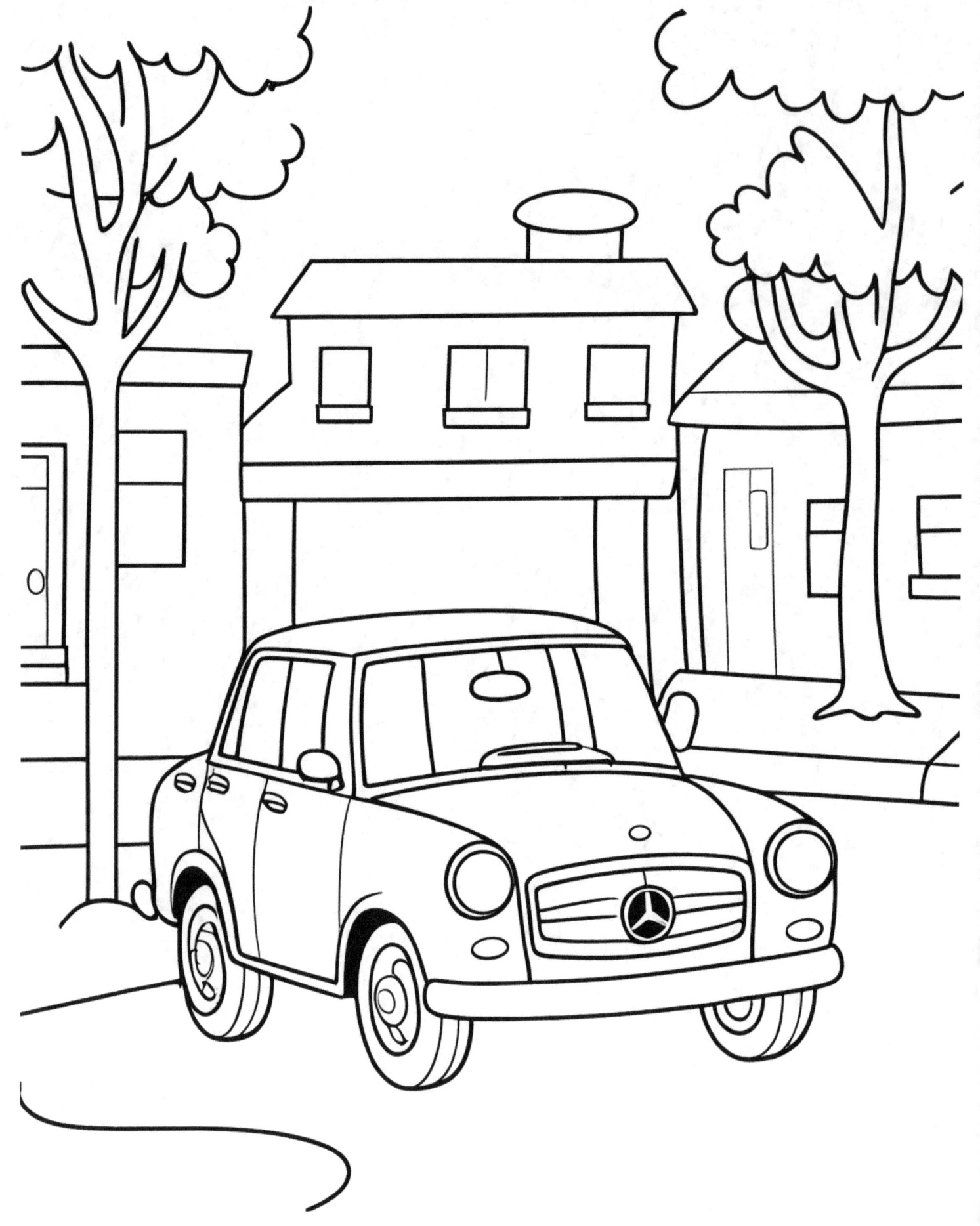

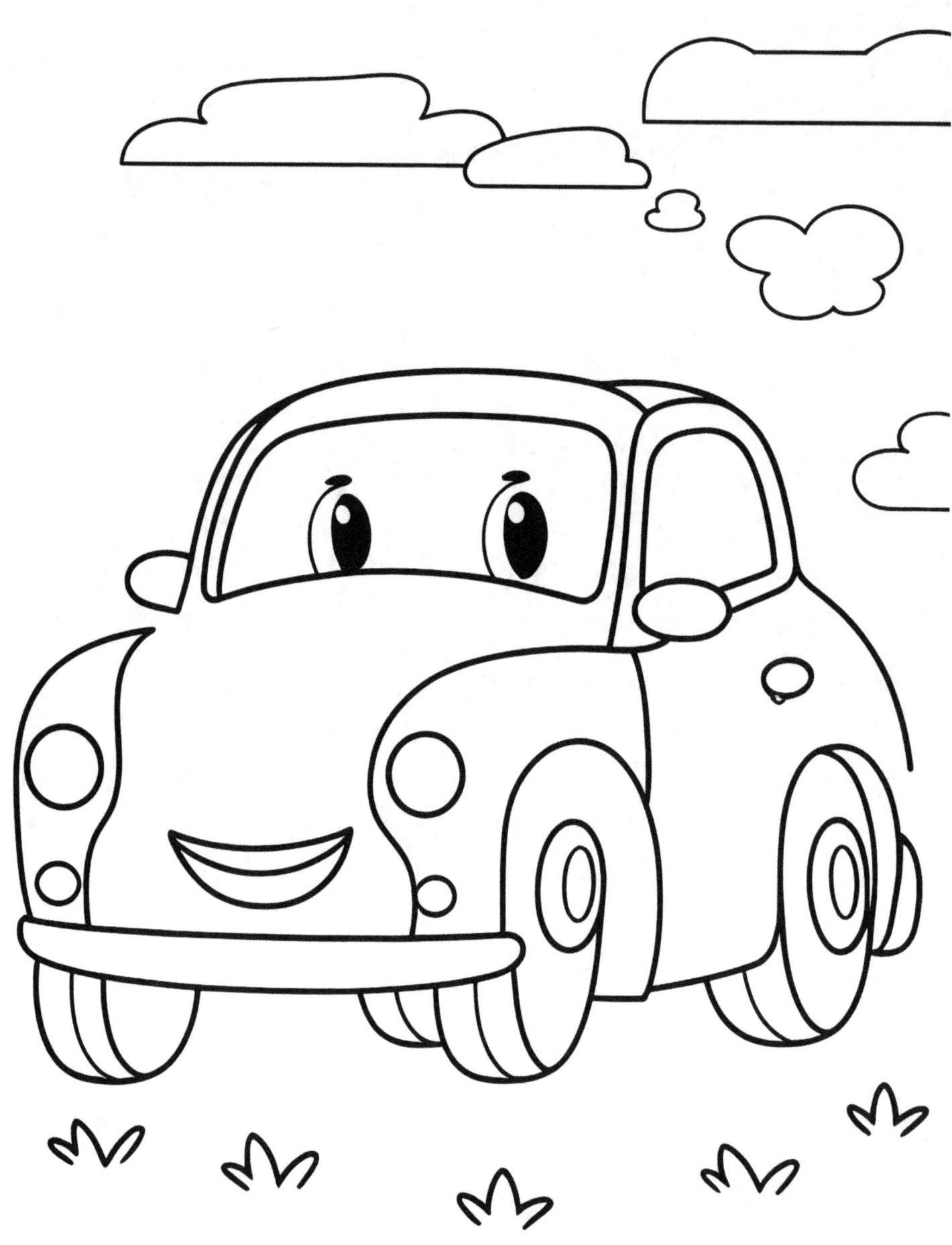

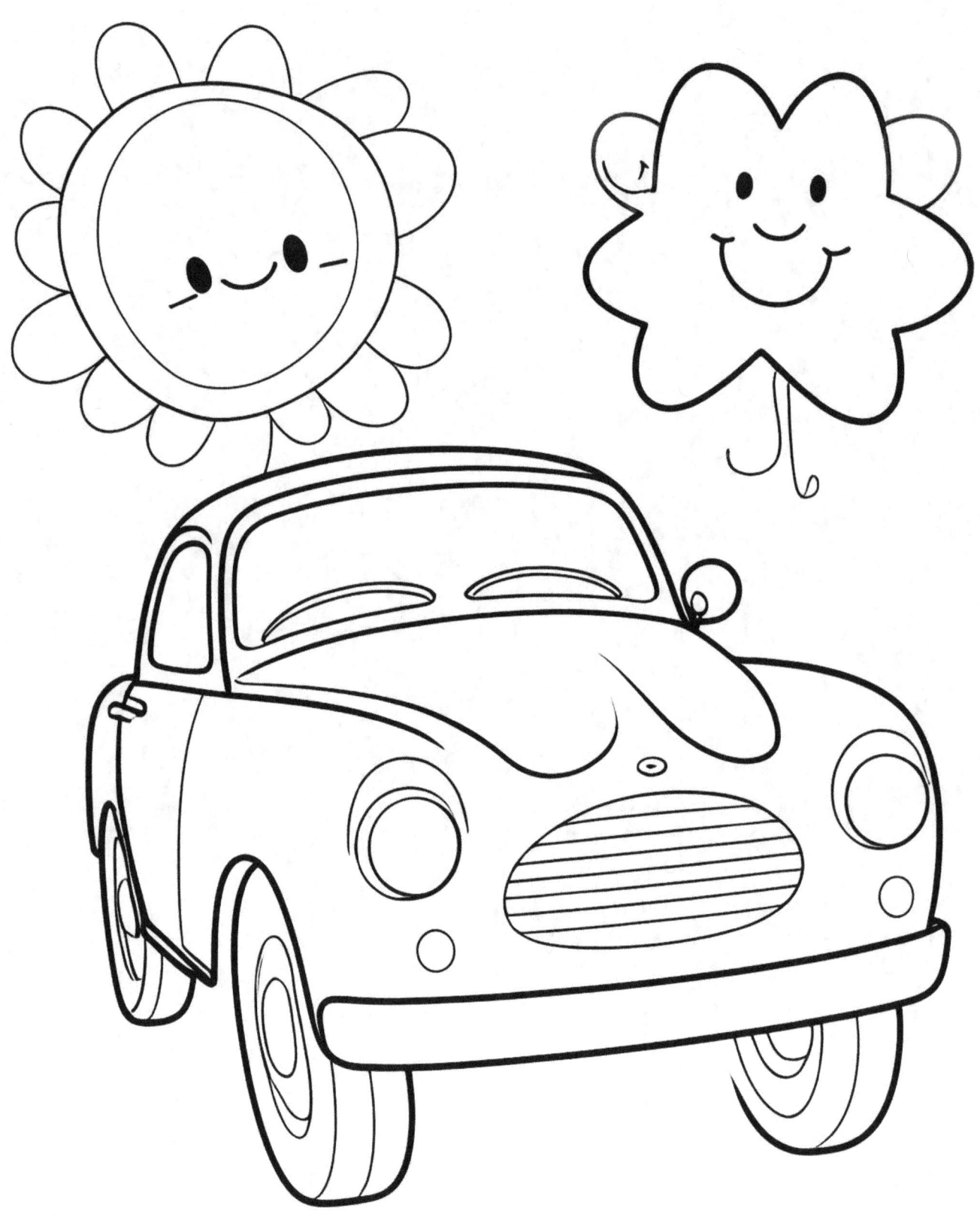

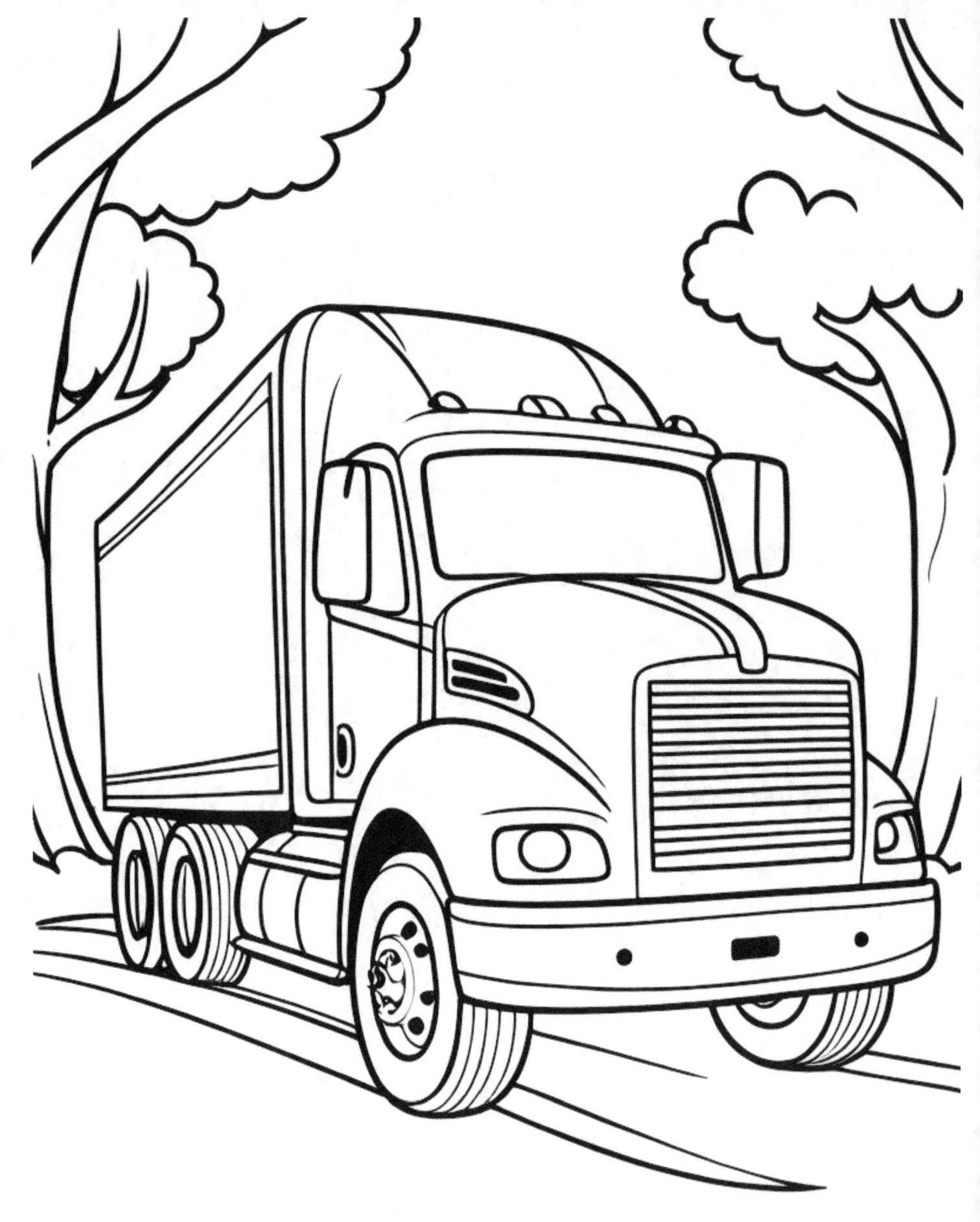

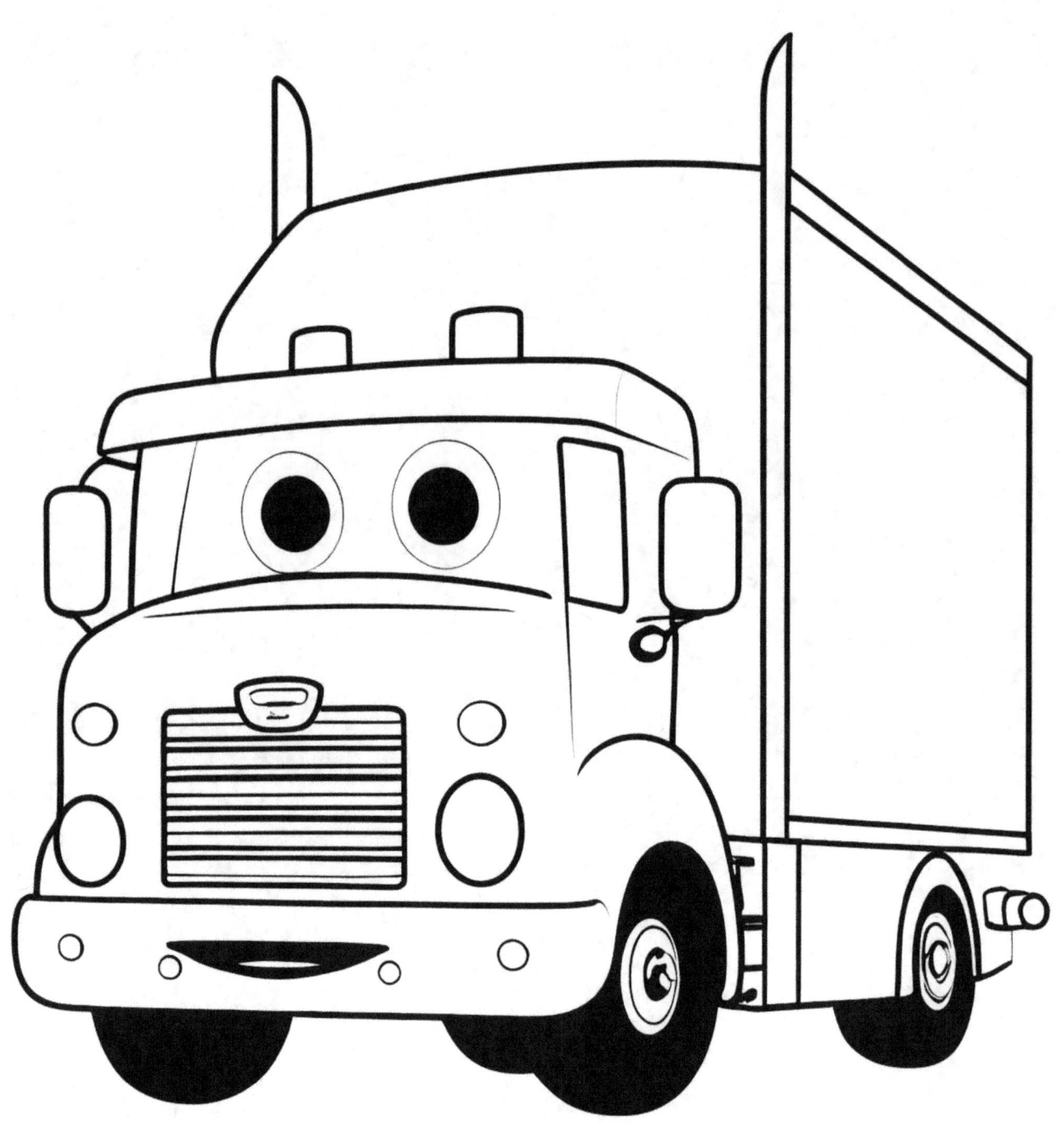

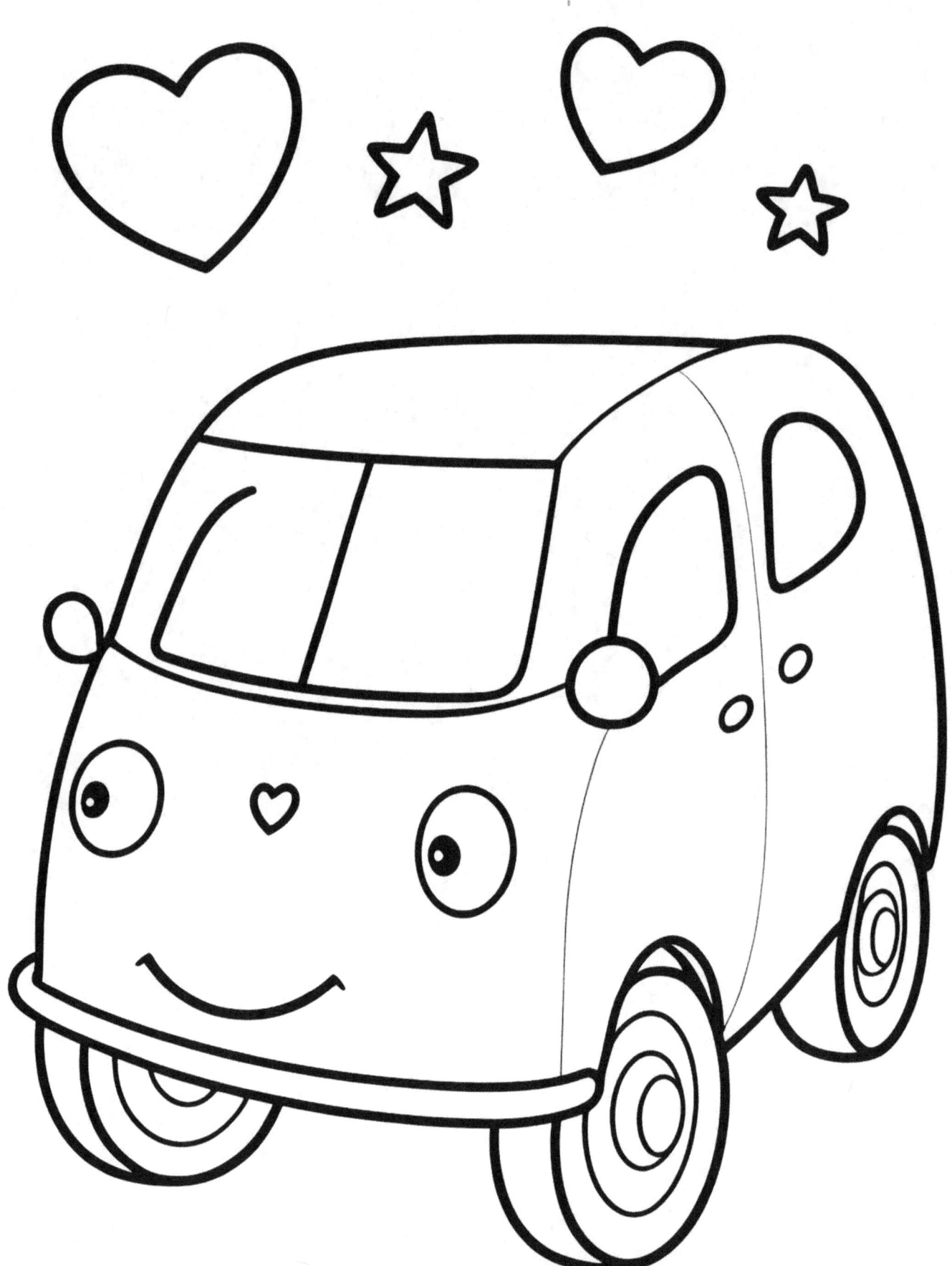

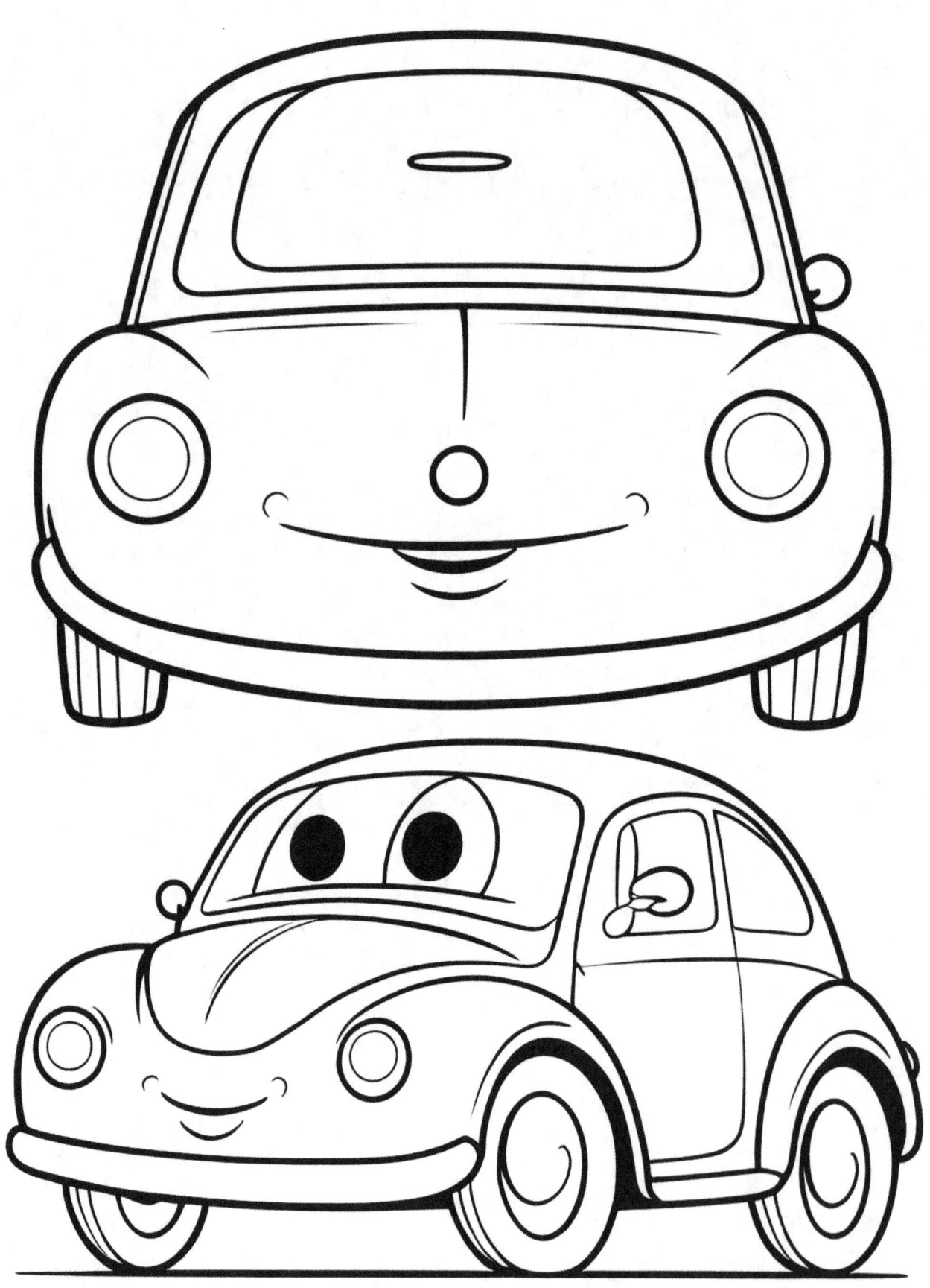

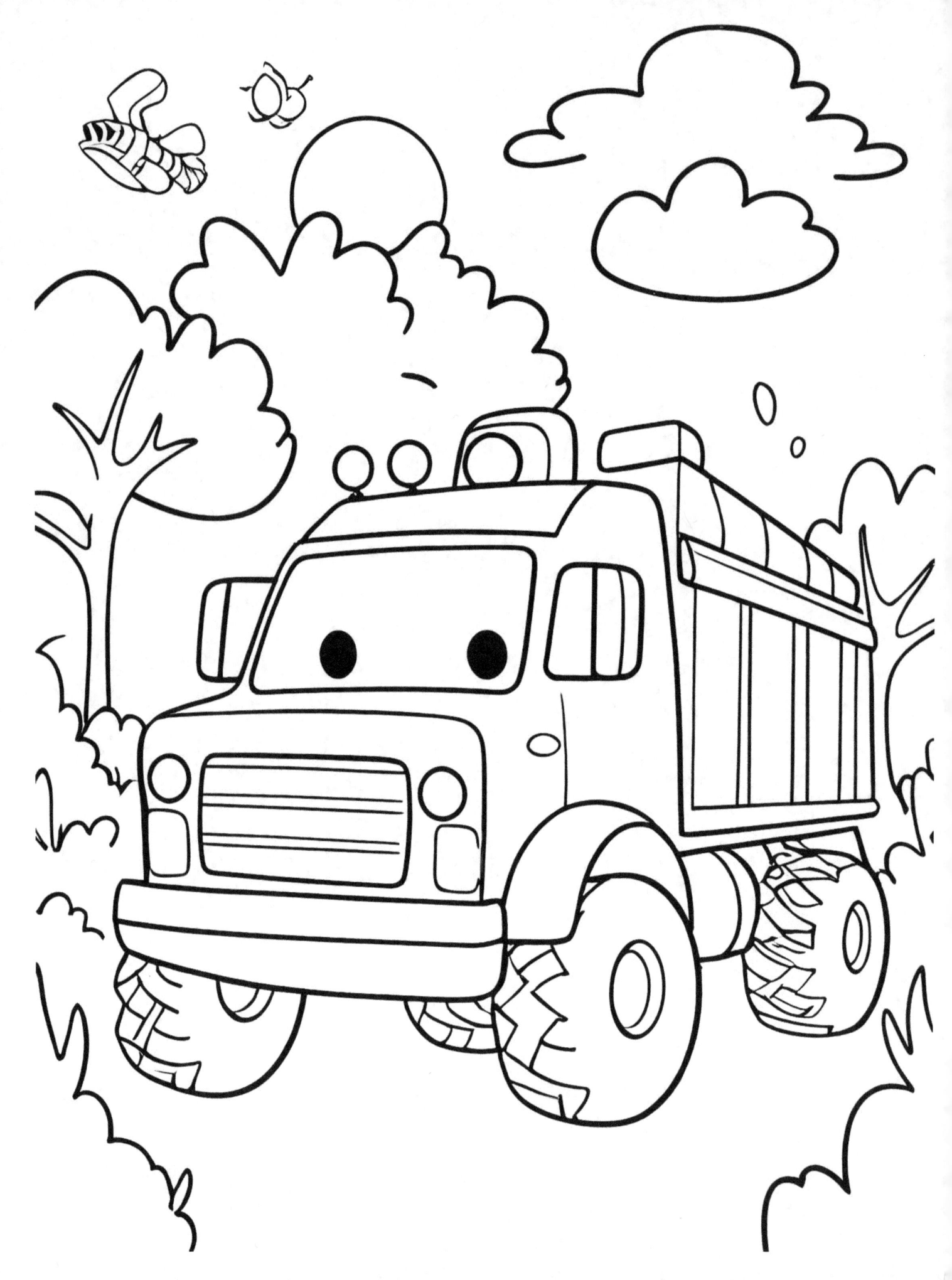